Appalachia Spring

Appalachia Spring

by Matthew Stevenson

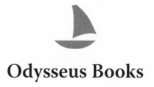

Odysseus Books

APPALACHIA SPRING.
Copyright © 2018 by Matthew Mills Stevenson.
ISBN-13: 978-0-9970580-0-0   ISBN-10: 0-9970580-0-5   (paperback)
ISBN-13: 978-0-9970580-1-7   ISBN-10: 0-9970580-1-3   (e-book)

For fulfillment information, address:
Odysseus Books c/o Pathway Book Service
34 Production Avenue, Keene, New Hampshire 03431.
Toll free: 1-800-345-6665. Tel: 1-603-357-0236.
Email: pbs@pathwaybook.com

Other inquiries: Odysseus Books.
Attention: David Wogahn, Publisher, publish@partnerpress.org

Please visit the book's Web site: www.odysseusbooks.com
To contact the author on any matter, such as to arrange a speaking engagement,
please use: matthewstevenson@sunrise.ch

Manufactured in the United States.
This book was printed on acid-free paper in the United States.
This paper meets the requirements of ANSI/NISO Z39.48-1992

Edited by Michael Martin, Robert Juran, and Deborah Bancroft.
Jacket and book design by Nanette Stevenson.

Library of Congress Cataloging-in-Publication Data
Stevenson, Matthew Mills, 1954–author.
Appalachia Spring/ by Matthew Stevenson.
p. cm. (Odysseus Books)
ISBN-13: 978-0-9970580-0-0 (cloth: alk. paper)
1. Stevenson, Matthew Mills, 1954—Travel. 2. Voyages and travels. I. Title.

---

10 9 8 7 6 5 4 3 2 1
First edition.

With enduring respect and admiration for:

TOM DEWEY, JEROME MARCUS, JON AUERBACH,
KARA SIEGEL, MAUREEN FITZGERALD, ARIEL CANNON,
TAMARA BOCK, DEBBIE KLEIN, WENDY SAPERSTONE,
JACOB GOLDBERG, MARTIN MENDELSOHN,
CHARLES PONCET, DANIELLE FALTER,
and JEAN-MARC CARNICÉ

*Without whom, Cicero might have been proved right
when he said: "When you have no basis for an argument,
abuse the plaintiff."*

And to ULLA HANSEVALL
A devoted friend to four generations of Stevensons

Contents

Foreword

SITTING IN A LAW OFFICE CONFERENCE ROOM, with a view of the Manhattan skyline and Queens, I decided to go to Appalachia. Lowering, angry clouds were whipping along the horizon of skyscrapers and, in the distance, row houses. Inside the conference room, I was into my second week of legal depositions, convened in a dispute that was in its sixth year and just getting around to hearing from witnesses.

The problem with American civil justice, at least for an individual plaintiff, is that it is hostage to corporate delays. Since filing the case in 2006, I had endured motions, briefs, cancellations, and arguments, all designed to drag out the case and make me give up from exhaustion. The case had wandered through various state and federal courthouses, several appeals, and motions for dismissal. They had failed to deter my claims, even if they dampened my spirits.

Now in the midst of defendant depositions, I had little to do, other than sit with a serious expression through testimony that invariably was marked by faulty memory or legal objections. The witnesses, all corporate hierarchs with whom I had worked for twenty-five years on nearly a daily basis, could hardly remember me, nor could they recall making promises about my pension that they failed to keep. When they could remember aspects of the case, it was only to claim that someone other than themselves were responsible for the sins of corporate omission or commission—even though the corporation had rewarded them with untold millions because, in theory, they were both honorable and trustworthy. It was therefore no surprise when the opposing lawyer arranged the schedule to my inconvenience, setting up depositions at the beginning and the end of April, leaving me with little choice, in the meantime, but to dream of the Appalachian spring.

With a court stenographer recording the statements and a videographer filming the witnesses, I decided to spend my down time on a drive across Virginia, Kentucky, and West Virginia, especially to the coal hollows that are at the juncture of the three states. I had not been to Appalachia since my senior year in high school, when I did an independent study project on the decline of American coal mines and spent two weeks on the train and bus riding around West Virginia. Now I live in Europe.

Not only did I want to return to the coal fields that are now forgotten in American politics—Robert Kennedy was the last national candidate to campaign seriously there—but on my way down and back I wanted to bike across some of the landscapes of the Civil War. In my conference-room doldrums I had imagined them fringed with flowering dogwoods, if not budding bluegrass. I thought that if I could ride around the contours of Chancellorsville, Appomattox, the Wilderness, or Perryville, I might set my own legal exhaustion in the context of other Americans who had to endure much more than the slings and arrows of lawyers or corporate intriguers.

* * *

Another reason that I had decided to head south-by-southwest from New York was that my mother was dying and I needed a respite, not just from the lawsuit, but from the ebb tide of her life, receding from an assisted-living room in Princeton, New Jersey. When not swearing to tell the whole truth and nothing but the truth, I had been with her, spending many days reading the newspaper aloud in her room or watching daytime television—where "Judge Judy" (Judith Sheindlin) was the chief justice. Had my own case ever been assigned to her televised courtroom, I often reflected, it would have been over in fifteen minutes, with the defendants ordered to pay me damages, not to mention two months' back rent. Leases and security deposits figure in many of Judge Judy's cases.

Although my mother had been slipping away for months, it was, nevertheless, comforting to spend hours in her company, even if she understood little of what I was saying or thinking. The expressions on her face still conveyed her depths of love and compassion, and it was easy for us to share the follies of Judge Judy's courtroom, especially as they were settled just in time for a commercial break. But not every moment in her room was filled with laughter, and in wanting to take in Appalachia's spring, I was also recalling happier times in her company, when she would celebrate winter's end in the company of blooming dogwoods.

For my route, I had only general ideas about waypoints. With more time, I might have tried for Tennessee and the Civil War battlefields at Shiloh and around Chattanooga. They lay over my horizon, so instead I set my sights on Appalachia. Before leaving, I collected maps and guidebooks about the

Civil War. From previous trips I knew Chancellorsville, the Wilderness, and Spotsylvania, but on this trip I wanted to stop in Fredericksburg, where at the end of 1862 the Union General Ambrose Burnside attacked uphill into entrenched Confederate lines, inviting slaughter. From Spotsylvania, I would head toward Appomattox, where the war ended, and continue to Roanoke, where in the old Norfolk & Western Railroad station is a museum dedicated to the train photographs of O. Winston Link, who prowled the branch lines of Virginia to record the vanishing era of steam engines.

From Roanoke, I wasn't sure where to cross the Cumberland Mountains, but wanted to head in the direction of Whitesburg, Kentucky, where the writer Harry M. Caudill had lived and worked as a local attorney. His books in the 1960s, especially *Night Comes to the Cumberlands*, had drawn the attention of the John F. Kennedy administration to the plight of what he called "a depressed area." From Whitesburg, I hoped to visit Harlan County and other Appalachian coalfields that live most vividly in folk ballads and literature. (Caudill recalls a local expression: "I was born with coaldust in my blood.")

From Hazard, where Robert F. Kennedy—just before he was killed—had come to bear witness to Appalachia in February 1968, I planned to drive as far into Kentucky as my time would allow and then double back across West Virginia. I knew I might have to stay in motels along the way, but I had hopes that the weather might cooperate so I could occasionally camp in the footprints of General Thomas Jonathan "Stonewall" Jackson, who had made his reputation across Virginia and its Shenandoah Valley. On the way home, I wanted to stop in Gettysburg long enough to bike the contours of the decisive 1863 battle.

I might only be gone a week or ten days, even less if summoned by the lawyers or my mother's health, but just the idea of escaping from Dante's legal circles and death's waiting rooms cheered me, and for once I didn't mind heading south on Interstate 95, the clogged artery of the American suburban empire.

Significantly, the one Yiddish word that has gained universal acceptance in this country is chutzpah. Example: In 1960, Mr. and Mrs. Podhoretz were in upstate New York where I used to live. I was trying out a play at the Hyde Park Playhouse; the play was set during the Civil War. "Why," asked Poddy, "are you writing a play about, of all things, the Civil War?" I explained to him that my mother's family had fought for the Confederacy and my father's for the Union, and that the Civil War was—and is—to the United States what the Trojan War was to the Greeks, the great single tragic event that continues to give resonance to our Republic.

—GORE VIDAL, *The Nation*, MARCH 22, 1986

"I was sick last year, and my friends in the Senate sent me a get-well card. The vote was 42 to 41."

—SENATOR ROBERT F. KENNEDY

"Yet Appalachia has now been so thoroughly bypassed and forgotten that it cannot give, because the rest of America will not take, what could be its greatest gift."

—HARRY M. CAUDILL, *Night Comes to the Cumberlands*

"They died for the most beautiful thing in the world—the dead South."

—F. SCOTT FITZGERALD

Appalachia Spring

Quantico, Virginia:
The real war will never get into the display cabinets

HEADING SOUTH FROM PRINCETON, New Jersey, to Fredericksburg, I decided to stop at the new Marine Corps Museum that straddles I-95 around Quantico, where the Marines train their officers and keep a university. I had done research at the previous Marine Corps museum, which was a collection of rifles and display cabinets tucked away behind a sentry point and uncertain hours at the Washington Navy Yard. The new museum, built at a cost of $90 million, is more in keeping with the expectations of a warrior nation. As I guided the car into the parking lot, I saw the sweeping atrium of steel and glass, built with the geometric symmetry of the Iwo Jima Memorial, which no doubt moonlights as a recruiting center for potential patriots adrift on the commuting tides of I-95.

Asking how to buy an entrance ticket, I fell into conversation with a man at the information kiosk. It turned out that I had a lot in common with Patrick Mooney, a museum curator. He had worked across the Pacific as a tour guide on cruise ships that took veterans back to places such as Okinawa and Guam, and from his voluminous reading of Marine Corps history he had come across my father's name in histories of the battles of Guadalcanal, Cape Gloucester, and Peleliu. Gregarious and chatty, he offered to walk me around the museum. For the next hour we strolled through Marine Corps history, beginning in the lobby at the recreated Tarawa seawall, where hundreds of casualties were suffered in the 1943 landings because planners miscalculated the tides and the location of the coral reef, leaving the Marines stranded in the crosshairs of Japanese rifles and mortars. A similar experience had awaited the Marines, including my father, at Peleliu, where the regimental commander, Lewis B. "Chesty" Puller, had told the men that, at most, all they would have to do after the landing was "police up the area with your bayonets." Instead, my father's 1st Battalion of the First Marine Regiment suffered a casualty rate that exceeded seventy percent.

Among the exhibits of the Pacific War, I told Patrick my story about General Ray Davis, who won the Medal of Honor for heroism during the retreat from the Chosin Reservoir in the Korean War. A four-star general by the end of his career, which spanned from World War II to Vietnam, Davis is mentioned in the museum dispatches, which prompted me to tell Patrick about Peleliu's Bloody Nose Ridge, where Davis commanded the 1st Battalion, First Marines, and my father was his executive officer, or second in command. The attack into the ridges and cliffs along Peleliu's spine had almost wiped out the 1st Battalion, including its C Company, which my father commanded for much of the war before Peleliu. On the fifth day of the near-futile fighting, Puller had ordered Davis to attack with what remained of the battalion into the teeth of the Japanese defenses, which were hidden throughout the hilltop caves. The orders bordered on the suicidal, although in the 1990s when I interviewed survivors of the battle, they liked to add, "For the attackers, not Puller."

Just before the dawn H-Hour, a runner approached my father, slightly to the rear of the battalion, and told him that Major Davis had been wounded and was turning over command of the battalion and the attack to him. My father rushed forward and saw the men (what was left of the battalion) ready to attack the Japanese on Bloody Nose Ridge. The enemy controlled the balconies of this deadly amphitheater, and the Marines were crawling around in the orchestra pit. He gave the order to move forward, although almost immediately the men were pinned down against coral escarpments and lay exposed to the rising sun and equatorial heat. He saw that continuing an assault with fewer than a hundred men, against fortified ridges, was folly, and sent word to regimental officers that the attack had stalled under withering Japanese fire. They continued holding their positions, but later that morning the 1st Battalion was relieved from the front lines, with only a few officers and a handful of men unwounded from the almost 1,000 Marines who had made the landing.

Whenever my father told me about that morning on Peleliu, he would bring up the last assault against Bloody Nose Ridge and the way he had been given command of the battalion. When the attack was called off and the battalion removed from the lines, he came across Davis, who showed no evidence of wounds. My father said: "But I never thought I needed to ask where he had been wounded. It just never came up." After a few days, Davis resumed command of the 1st Battalion, which for the remainder of its time on Peleliu was held in reserve away from the deadly ridges. For the rest of his life, my father wondered why Davis left the fighting at that critical time.

After traveling to Peleliu in 1994, I searched around for material about the attack on Bloody Nose Ridge. I interviewed survivors, consulted historians at the old Marine Corps museum, and wrote to dozens of veterans, including General Davis. In the days before Internet book searches, I managed to track down several histories about Peleliu—notably James Hallas's *The Devil's Anvil: The Assault on Peleliu*—and several memoirs. The best was *Marine at War* by Russell Davis, no relation to the general, who, I discovered, had also published his memoirs, *The Story of Ray Davis*. These books piled up in my home office. As I read them, I discussed the contents with my father, who liked to fill in between the historical lines with more colorful accounts of fellow officers and their foibles. For example, before Davis took command of the 1st Battalion, the commander had been Colonel John Warner, who, because he was morose, had been given the nickname "Jolly Jack."

When I tracked down a copy of Ray Davis's memoirs, I thought for sure he would explain how he was wounded beneath Bloody Nose Ridge and the change of command. As I read the chapter in the memoir, it shed no light on either question. It omitted the episode altogether and focused instead on my father's successor as commander of C Company, Everett Pope, who had won the Medal of Honor on nearby Hill 100. Nor did General Davis clear up this fog of war when I wrote to him, which he answered by adding marginalia to my letter, as if I had sent him an office memo.

There the matter stood until I figured out that in writing his memoir about Bloody Nose Ridge, Davis had plagiarized word-for-word the corresponding section in the Hallas book.

The four-star general had purloined passages that go on for pages. Everett Pope, who was a good friend both to Davis and my father, said: "He did not just copy a few sentences. He lifted the entire chapter."

At first it wasn't clear to me whether Hallas had copied from Davis or Davis from Hallas. A quick look at the publication dates made it clear that Davis had stolen his chapter from Hallas. When I wrote to Davis and raised the similarity of the accounts, he wrote back, again in the margin, "I don't understand what you are talking about?" I wrote to Hallas, living in Connecticut, who acknowledged that the general and Medal of Honor winner had lifted entire pages of his book and passed them off as part of his own memoir.

In his letter, Hallas confessed that he was upset at the plagiarism but didn't know what he could do about it. Davis was a four-star general now in retirement and one of the greatest legends in the history of the Corps. I suggested that maybe Hallas's publisher should seek an apology, but he said it had no interest in pursuing the claim. Later I heard that Davis's ghostwriter on the memoir project was angry over something and had sued the general, although I never heard whether it was the plagiarism or another issue. A plagiarized memoir raises many questions about what the author wants to remember or forget. A few years after all this, I read that Davis had died, putting to rest that side of the story.

Walking around the new Marine Corps Museum with Patrick Mooney, who admired Davis and had even traveled with him in the Pacific, made me wonder how any museum can capture all the avenues of history. The elegant display cabinets are better at what H.G. Wells called "the outline of history," explaining the winners and the losers, and showcasing those, including Ray Davis, who were awarded congressional medals. Nevertheless, there is another side of history that will never get into the dioramas—those ambiguities of battle Stephen Crane describes.

Even today I don't know whether, in leading the hopeless attack against Bloody Nose Ridge, Davis got cold feet and headed to the rear—a lapse of nerve in a military career that was otherwise one of the finest in the history of the country. He easily could have been stunned by a shell. I do know, however, that when it came time to tell this story in his memoirs, he chose to gloss over the details of the incident and insert pages from another man's book. The World War I British poet Siegfried Sassoon, himself a veteran of many front-line trenches, writes in "Glory of Women":

> *You can't believe that British troops 'retire'*
> *When hell's last horror breaks them, and they run,*
> *Trampling the terrible corpses—blind with blood.*

Fredericksburg, Virginia:
" . . . so terrible, or we should grow too fond of it"

FROM QUANTICO, I HEADED TOWARD Fredericksburg and its national battlefield park, although by mid-afternoon the lines of cars on the interstate resembled an army in retreat, if only from Washington cubicles. I pulled up to the visitor center shortly before it closed, but had enough time to watch the short film about the battle and to collect a map that indicated a park road running along the Confederate lines, which were dug into the hillsides overlooking the Rappahannock River. Crossing the river in the depths of winter and attacking up the enfiladed slopes brought the same defeat and slaughter to the Union armies that the Confederates would experience on the last day of Gettysburg.

Because I had my bike in the back of the car, I changed into my riding clothes in the outdoor men's room and headed off in the direction of the Sunken Road, so prominent in histories of the battle. Among those that crossed the river and started up the hill toward the Confederate lines, only to be pinned down under withering fire, was Joshua Lawrence Chamberlain, whose 20th Maine Regiment saved the second day on Little Round Top at Gettysburg. At Fredericksburg, however, he spent the cold night of the attack huddled against a man who turned out to be dead, waiting for a moment to retreat back down the hillside. Chamberlain writes:

> At last, outwearied and depressed with the desolate scene, my own strength sunk, and I moved two dead men a little and lay down between them, making a pillow of the breast of a third. The skirt of his overcoat drawn over my face helped also to shield me from the bleak winds. There was some comfort even in this companionship. But it was broken sleep. The deepening chill drove many forth to take the garments of those who could no longer need them, that they might keep themselves alive. More than once I was startled from my unrest by someone turning back the coat skirt from my face, peering, half vampire-like, to my fancy, through the darkness, to discover if it too were of the silent and unresisting; turning away more disconcerted at my living word than if a voice had spoken from the dead.

In the springtime sunset it looked nothing like the fortified killing field that it was in December 1862, when the Union commanding general, Ambrose Burnside, ordered his divisions across the river and up the entrenched hill. Despite the cold and the moving waters of the Rappahannock, he had ordered pontoon bridges to span the river—the first place the Confederates concentrated their fire.

The uphill side of the Sunken Road—now restored to park splendor although still evocative of the desperate struggle—offered the attacking Union soldiers something of a respite from the fire coming down the hill, much the same way that, at Normandy's Omaha Beach, the first waves huddled against the seawall under the bluffs.

General George Pickett commanded the Confederate division on top of what is called Marye's Heights, to which I walked without my bike. I doubt even modern mechanized troops could have carried out a successful attack under such conditions. Many pontoon bridges were destroyed. Once the Union forces were across the river, they lay like sitting ducks under the eyes of Pickett's men on the heights. A cemetery lines much of Marye's Heights. It is a place Union soldiers reached only in death, as few crested the lines on the hilltop. I walked among the headstones and springtime dogwoods, and then returned to my bike to ride out of Fredericksburg along what is called Lee's Road.

While Pickett guarded Marye's Heights in the town of Fredericksburg, Lee had arranged his other divisions along a ridge that ran to the south and parallel to the Rappahannock River. He knew that Burnside would attempt to cross the river at several points, and he divided the lines among his corps commanders—generals James Longstreet and Thomas "Stonewall" Jackson, his most experienced lieutenants. They arranged their men in the woods and rolling hills that overlooked the river from a distance of about a thousand yards. Lee himself selected a hilltop near General Longstreet's men from which to command the battle. That perch, where I rode with my bike, has the feel of an eagle's nest. Although the surrounding trees have grown up around the encampment in the intervening 150 years, in Lee's time he had a sweeping view of the fighting. It was here that he uttered his melancholic observation on battle. "It is well," he remarked, "that war is so terrible, or we should grow too fond of it."

According to a brochure, the battlefield closed at sunset, but no one was around to keep me from riding along the park road, which had signs showing the limits of Longstreet's command and others pointing the way to the vestiges of some trenches. I reached the end of the road at Prospect Hill, took pictures of cannons pointed toward the river, imagined the forces of General Meade making some headway against the Confederates until they closed the lines, and then rode back toward the visitor center as the sun set through the trees on Marye's Heights. Having seen the Heights, I could not imagine what had possessed Burnside to carry out his frontal attacks against such an entrenched enemy and up such steep hills. At least at Normandy the amphibious troops had the support of air and naval squadrons, not to mention paratroops and, eventually, tanks. I could now understand why my father, on his trips around the South, was so drawn to the futility of Marye's Heights, and how they must have reminded him of Peleliu's Bloody Nose Ridge.

At Fredericksburg, all Burnside's men had were their muskets and bayonets, neither of which reached very far up the slopes. After the loss (or deadly draw) at Antietam Creek in September 1862, Lincoln replaced General George McClellan with Burnside, hoping for a decisive battle with Lee's army. While he, more than his predecessor, was eager for battle, Burnside lacked Lee's battlefield vision or even Jackson's ruthless determination. Instead, he assembled his army for a slaughter without too many critical questions about what proved to be a hopeless plan. Ulysses S. Grant, who later used Burnside as a corps commander, said of him that he "was an officer who was generally liked and respected. He was not, however, fitted to command an army. No one knew this better than himself." After Fredericksburg, Lincoln selected "Fighting Joe" Hooker to command his army along the Rappahannock. Both generals would give more to American slang than they would to military greatness—Burnside for his facial hair and Hooker for his choice of evening company.[1]

By the time I had changed my clothes and returned the bike to the trunk of the car, it was well after dark and I had yet to find a place to stay for the night. The ranger at the visitor center had marked a map for me, explaining that downtown Fredericksburg had some restaurants and inns for the night. I had dinner in a restaurant near the railroad station, sitting at one of those elevated tables with high stools around it. Because it was too dark to read, I watched baseball on one of the bar's five large screens, which surrounded me with staccato images of basketball, baseball, and hockey.

After dinner, I had no luck finding the inn marked on the map, and took a chance on finding "something" closer to Chancellorsville, about eight miles west, where I planned to start the next day. I even had it in mind to camp somewhere near the battlefields, provided I could find an open campground. Because I was there before the summer season, however, everything was closed. Nor did I want to risk pitching my tent in some farmer's field. That left me no choice but to return to the interstate exit, and choose from the motels clustered around gas stations, McDonald's, and ice cream parlors—the Conestoga wagons of the new frontier. I pitched up to a Day's Inn that, instead of a campfire, had two enormous

---

1: A better nickname for Fighting Joe would have been "Organization Man" Hooker, as he was better at maintaining the details of armies than he was in the rush of battle.

king-sized beds covered with what felt like an infield tarpaulin in floral patterns. At least I could have comforted General Lee: such accommodations were nothing I would ever "grow too fond of."

Chancellorsville, Virginia:
The most famous flanking movement in U.S. history

When I woke up to a drenching rain, I was glad not to be camping, although breakfast at the Waffle House made me nostalgic for something other than industrial-strength coffee served in thick-sided mugs. I had paid the bill for the motel when I checked in, so I left for Chancellorsville directly from breakfast, following the Plank Road (a good Civil War name) in the direction of the Old Salem Church, where Union and Confederate forces fought a battle on May 3, 1863, a decisive day around Chancellorsville.

The house and small museum were closed, so I poked around the grounds in the rain, discouraged because today was not one for riding on a bike from Chancellorsville to Spotsylvania. Lee had better luck at the Old Salem Church. With his forces fighting around Chancellorsville, he had divided his army and turned back toward Fredericksburg, where John Sedgwick's men had finally taken Marye's Heights and were advancing to join Hooker at Chancellorsville. Lee dispatched General Lafayette McLaws to confront the advancing Union army, which was defeated and chased across the Rappahannock. Hooker would end up there as well after the battle for

Chancellorsville, prompting President Lincoln to say of the defeats: "My god! What will the country say?"

I escaped the rain inside the Chancellorsville Visitor Center and sat through the filmstrip explanation of the fighting around the crossroads and the Chancellor family home. Hooker had thought that by crossing the river above Fredericksburg he would surprise Lee, deal a knockout blow to the Confederates, and march victorious on Richmond to end the war.[2] Against the combination of Lee and Jackson, however, Hooker had little chance, especially after the two Confederate generals scratched out a plan in the dirt that sent Jackson on the most famous flanking movement in U.S. military history.

After the visitor center, I drove in the car to the spot where Lee and Jackson had hatched their plan to deliver a left hook into Hooker's men, who were cooking meals and drying laundry rather than expecting Jackson's force to burst from the forest on their right. After the plan was agreed at the small crossroads near Chancellorsville—marked with a plaque, although it looks like a Boy Scout campsite—Jackson led his men twelve miles on a dirt path that encircled the Union right front. From the dust on the horizon, Hooker and his staff saw that Jackson was on the move but chose to believe that Lee had ordered him to retreat. The Union general said: "I have Lee just where I want him." In Napoleonic terms, however, Hooker was "painting pictures." He should have known that Jackson didn't go to war to lead retreats.

2: "My plans are perfect," Hooker said. "If the enemy doesn't run, God help them," to which the more cautious Lincoln responded: "The hen should lay eggs before cackling."

General Oliver Howard, whose loose flank ("floating in the air") Jackson had attacked at Chancellorsville, described what happened next: "More quickly than it could be told, with all the fury of the wildest hailstorm, everything, every sort of organization that lay in the path of the mad current of panic-stricken men had to give way and be broken into fragments." Another Union soldier said, "The whole army has gone to pieces." Ironically, had Hooker attacked into the gap between Lee and Jackson after seeing the dust on the horizon, he might well have rolled up the Army of Northern Virginia and ended the Civil War.

With Chancellorsville in the bag, however, Lee would be emboldened to march north, first to Chambersburg and then Gettysburg. It is safe to say that Jackson's victory at Chancellorsville gave the Confederates several more years of war, although it came at the cost of his own life. That evening at dusk, scouting the front lines, Jackson was shot by some of his own men, and he died a week later, after doctors moved him away from the fighting to a small plantation office in Guinea Station, Virginia. (The site is visible from Amtrak trains heading north from Richmond.)

On my drive, I passed signs for the route that the mortally wounded Jackson followed in his ambulance. If to the Confederate army Jackson's life was as celebrated as that of Jesus—the general had qualities of religious mysticism about him, as well as dogged determination and kindly affection for his men— the roadside markers read like the Stations of the Cross. As he left the battlefield, Lee wept: "He has lost his left arm, and I have lost my right arm." (Jackson's amputated arm would be buried separately from his body.) According to legend, Jackson's last words were, "No, no, let us cross over the river and rest under the shade of the trees." A century later, Ernest Hemingway would use these words as a title for his novel—set in Venice, although about the disastrous World War II battle in the Huertgen Forest—*Across the River and into the Trees.*

The Wilderness:
"Lee's army, and not Richmond, is your true objective"

HAD THE SUN SHONE ON MY PLANS, I would have started biking in Chancellorsville and taken the small park roads from the Wilderness battlefields to Spotsylvania Court House, where in 1864, after assuming command of the Union's Army of the Potomac, General Grant would turn his forces toward Richmond and fight a series of battles that bled both armies to near exhaustion. I would have poked along the preserved lanes, stopped for pictures, and read the inscriptions on the plaques about Chewning or Trapp farm—some of the eventful engagements. Instead, the hard rains continued, and I made the tour in the car, parking near monuments to read explanations that began with simple words, such as "Hell Itself."

In comparing Chancellorsville to the Huertgen Forest, Hemingway got his analogy wrong. Chancellorsville was the last of the Napoleonic battles in North America, fought with dashing cavalry rides and influenced by charismatic command, notably Jackson's. By contrast, the Wilderness was a prelude to the world wars of the twentieth century, when armies sometimes did little more than march into hailstorms of fire. In the Huertgen Forest, which is south of Aachen and close to the Rhine River, U.S. commanders between September and December 1944 poured division after division into what was called a "dark and bloody land." Such was the density of the trees that mortars often exploded in the treetops, which further distributed their deadly shrapnel on the foxholes below. Although the Wilderness was fought without mortars or tanks, neither would have penetrated far into the undergrowth that devoured Grant's attacking divisions and reduced regiments to clusters of men, sometimes not much larger than platoons or squads.

When the rain had lessened, I stopped the car near the intersection of the Plank and Block roads, and followed marked trails into the woods. At a memorial for the Vermont Brigade, I noted that in two days of fighting in the forests— May 5 and 6, 1864—it had suffered 1,234 casualties, which is more than any American division endured in all the fighting in Iraq or Afghanistan over ten years. A plaque in the forest recalls the words of an articulate Union staff officer, Robert Robertson: "The woods would light up with the flashes of musketry, as if with lightning, while the incessant roar of the volleys sounded like the crashing of thunder-bolts. Brave men were falling like autumn leaves, and death was holding high carnival in our ranks."

When the fighting subsided on May 6, Grant had fared no better than Burnside at Fredericksburg or Hooker at Chancellorsville, in that he had lost thousands of men and left Lee in control of his defenses. The repeated pattern of Union generalship would have called for Grant to withdraw across the Rappahannock and for Lincoln to channel the eloquence of a poet such as Walt Whitman in decrying the hunger of the war gods. Instead, Grant, who found backtracking personally distasteful ("I will take no backward step"), shifted his men slightly to the east and headed south around Lee's division, in a race for Spotsylvania Court House.

Such a jug-handle move did not change the outcome in the Wilderness—at best a bloody stalemate, if not a shared defeat—but it did give Grant's troops a better sense of their new commander and the feeling that he was in the war to end it. (He summed up his battlefield motto this way: "Find out where your enemy is. Get at him as soon as you can, and strike him as hard as you can. And keep moving on!") If Jackson's flanking movement gave the Confederacy several more years of warring life, Grant's sidestep out of the Wilderness was the first move in that general's end game.

Later, an attrition strategy—because he had more men to lose than Lee did—was attributed to Grant's grand designs, although as I was driving down Highway 613 to Spotsylvania Court House I wondered if he was that precise when he commanded his men to move around Lee and head south. Grant did, however, buy into Lincoln's strategy, which the president had earlier expressed to Hooker: "I think Lee's army, and not Richmond, is your true objective." Previous Union commanders assumed Richmond was the objective and when it fell the rebellion would be finished. Until the end of the war almost a year later, Grant would do nothing but batter Lee's forces head-on, a strategic legacy bequeathed to American generals in the Argonne Forest (WW I) and on Okinawa (WW II), where it earned the macabre designation "Straight ahead into the sausage machine."

Nevertheless, for all that General Grant is associated with orders to attack directly into the enemy—as he had at

Shiloh, with horrific casualties—Grant the man found few pleasures in wars or in fighting them. Lee, who was a tactical genius especially during the fighting, would have felt the thrill of war as he positioned his men around the glades and forests of the Wilderness. It was there he would also have missed the dynamic of shared emotions with his departed lieutenant, "Stonewall" Jackson; and one way to interpret Confederate losses in 1864–65 is to analyze how out of sync Lee was with Jackson's replacements, especially James Longstreet, who thrived on the defensive. For Grant on his way to Spotsylvania, where more casualties awaited his army, my guess is that the only emotion he would have felt was a kind of existential calm that allowed him to see clarity on battlefields when others saw only carnage.

Spotsylvania:
"The place was well named the Bloody Angle"

THE RAIN PAUSED WHEN I GOT TO SPOTSYLVANIA, so I
parked the car and reassembled the bike, with the idea of riding through the battlefield park on what a map called Grant
Drive. I kept on the bike even after I bumped into a park
ranger who said he was organizing a 1 p.m. tour of the Bloody
Angle, where Union forces (as if in a dress rehearsal for World
War I) repeatedly attacked a fortified Confederate trench,
suffering thousands of casualties as they made their way forward armed with no more than bayonets and war cries.[3]

The ranger was happy for me to join the tour because
the rain meant few visitors were lurking about the battlefield,
although I regretted the guided excursion when he began
speaking to us in the weary voice of a burdened civil servant.
Leading tours around a Civil War battlefield park cannot be
one of the harder jobs in government service, but by his exas-
perated tone I sensed that what he most liked to do was visit
the hallowed fields by himself—a sentiment I shared after

3: Before the battle, Confederate Brigadier General Albert Perrin said: "I shall come
out of this fight a live major general or a dead brigadier." He was killed in action.

staring at a landscape unburdened with monuments and, by its stillness, speaks volumes for the war's sacred nothingness.

A salient in Confederate lines at Spotsylvania, nicknamed "the mule shoe," drew repeated futile attacks from the Union forces. Men marched or rushed directly into the meat grinder. The most innovative attack came under the command of Union Colonel Emory Upton, who, instead of marching his men with arms locked together into the Confederate trenches, chose to line them up in four columns and have them punch narrow holes into the defensive lines.

As a lesson in military theory, Upton's experiment would be lost to history until the late stages of World War I, when Allied commanders adopted similar tactics to breach holes in German trench lines. At Spotsylvania, however, Upton's innovation with 5,000 men was ignored and no reinforcements came forward to exploit his breakthrough. Later waves against the salient spread the men abreast, as Napoleon would have, and the consequence is that Confederate cannons blew wide swaths through the Union ranks.

After the tour, I biked along most of the park's road and headed to the car only when the rains resumed. For me, Spotsylvania remains one of the haunted hallows of the Civil War, as it seems little changed in the last 150 years. The salients in Lee's lines are easy to imagine, and there is a melancholy to the woods that evokes another passage from Stephen Crane: "It was not well to drive men into final corners; at those moments they could all develop teeth and claws."

Casualties between May 5 and May 21, 1863, were 36,000 Union soldiers and 24,000 Confederates, equal to one in three of all men engaged on both sides. In a visit to the battlefield just after the fighting ended, Union Colonel Horace Porter wrote:

> The appalling sight presented was harrowing in the extreme. Our own killed were scattered over a large space near the 'angle,' while in front of the captured breastworks the enemy's dead . . . were piled upon each other in some places four layers deep, exhibiting every ghastly phase of mutilation. Below the mass of fast-decaying corpses, the convulsive twitching of limbs and the writhing of bodies showed that there were wounded men still alive and struggling to extricate themselves from their horrid entombment. Every relief possible was afforded, but in too many cases came too late. The place was well named the 'Bloody Angle.'

Yet for all that suffering, Grant could not claim Spotsylvania as a victory, except for its body counts. Nevertheless, he continued to march south, and by such sacrifices ("the dead covered more than five acres of ground about as thickly as they could be laid") he pinned Lee into the corner of southern Virginia.

Appomattox, Virginia:
Orange Blossom Special

BECAUSE I WANTED TO SPEND THE NIGHT in Appomattox, where the war ended in April 1865, I devised a route that cut south by southwest across central Virginia. The drive from Spotsylvania would take two to three hours, as I planned to take back roads through such evocative places as Mineral, Louisa, Fork Union, Bremo Bluff, Dillwyn, and Sprouses Corner. By contrast, after the battle, Grant had taken another sidestep east and headed toward Richmond on the line that I-95 now follows to the south. I had thought about a visit to the battlefields around Richmond, notably Cold Harbor, where Grant again sacrificed a large percentage of his army. The war's end at Appomattox had more appeal, and headed me in the direction of the Kentucky coal fields. Not only had I never been to Appomattox, but I also wanted to see Roanoke and the coal counties of southwest Virginia.

Driving through rain and clouds toward Appomattox and listening on and off to the car radio, I kept hearing strange sounds, as though my cell phone were trying to ring or the range of radio was stretched to its limits. At the same time, the skies had turned a dark color I had never seen before.

The clouds were low and menacing, and threw off both mists and bands of showers that felt like bursts of hail. Finally, I listened closely to the car radio and it dawned on me that I was hearing warnings of the emergency broadcast system, which was signaling a line of powerful tornadoes on the border of Virginia and North Carolina, slightly to the east of where I was driving.

As I live in Europe, I had lost touch with the sounds of the emergency alarms. The tones were followed with static-filled broadcasts that indicated the latitude and longitude of the twisters, which looked as if they could well be on my horizon. Figuring that this was nature's way of telling me it was time for a late lunch, I pulled into a barbecue shack, where the waitress served me pulled pork, cole slaw, and root beer, and told of the many deaths the storms had caused the night before in North Carolina. As rain and wind slashed the parking lot, I lingered more than an hour in my booth. When I got back on the road to Appomattox, I was pleased to drive through late-afternoon sunshine and an evocative landscape on Highway 24 between Mt. Rush and Appomattox. At the very least, Lee and Grant had chosen a beautiful corner of America in which to end their differences.

Appomattox Court House is on Highway 24 just outside the new town of Appomattox, which decamped from its Civil War location in the nineteenth century and moved closer to the railroad station. The place where Lee surrendered to Grant is now part of a national historic park, although one that feels like a Disneyland exhibition, perhaps one featuring wax figures that speak in the voices of Civil War generals. When I got there, around 5:30 p.m., the park was unofficially still open. I took a walk down the main street and greeted some Civil War re-enactors, complete with uniforms, muskets, and cannons, who were gathering at a bivouac within the park. The shops and museums were closed, so I pushed on to the new town, hoping I might not have a long search for a motel or an inn.

The new town of Appomattox—which saw fighting around the railroad station when Union troops burned the last of Lee's supply trains—has strips of drug stores and waffle houses on its edges. The small downtown section around the station, however, has historic houses and buildings, including a number selling antiques. I didn't see any hotels or campgrounds on the drive into town, so I parked at the railroad station. Finding the visitor center closed, I went across the street to Baine's Books and Coffee to ask directions for a place to stay.

The shop's owner, a cheerful man setting up for an evening concert, told me the area had no campgrounds. Then he asked: did I really want to camp with tornadoes on the loose? He suggested I try to get a room at the Longacre Bed & Breakfast, on the other side of the tracks. He also said the café would be open that evening for dinner, to sell books, and for bluegrass music—all of which interested me. Looking around the store, I mentally staked out a place for my dinner, in one of the oversized easy chairs near the books about the Civil War. I felt like I was home.

Promising to come back, I drove to the bed and breakfast, met the owner, and was shown into a second floor bedroom fit, if not for a king, then at least a Civil War general. It had a canopy bed, a desk for my computer, a divan with a reading light, and a selection of bottled waters.

Even though it was Saturday night, I was the only guest in the house, and the owner told me to lock up when she left to visit her daughter. By now the clouds were gone, and the evening had turned warm. As much as I wanted to settle into my divan with a book and a cup of tea, I roused myself from my comforts and biked to the bookstore for dinner and the bluegrass concert. The chance to hear live music was too good to miss, and I spent the evening browsing among the books and listening to the banjoes. One of the musicians sang "Orange Blossom Special"—*I'll ride that Orange Blossom Special/And lose these New York blue*s—and I found it sad that no passenger trains had come to Appomattox since the 1970s.

Appomattox Court House, Virginia:
"I would rather die a thousand deaths"

BEFORE BREAKFAST THE NEXT MORNING, sensing that I might have a break in the bad weather, I got up early to bike back to the historic courthouse and to see the surrounding battlefield sites. The woods near Appomattox Court House are where Lee had his headquarters on the last day of his command. In early April 1865, he had executed a fighting retreat on the line from Richmond to Appomattox, with the hope of turning south into North Carolina and uniting his army with that of General Joseph E. Johnston, then being pushed by General William T. Sherman north from Atlanta. Although the world assumes that Lee moved west of Richmond and Petersburg with the understanding that the war would soon be over, he certainly didn't lead the troops as if the end were near. At Sailor's Creek he turned back to attack the stalking Union army, and that forgotten battle of the Civil War left some 7,000 casualties on both sides, a week before the surrender. So much for mailing in his resignation.

The house where Lee surrendered to Grant is now a replica of the McLean homestead where the two men and their staffs gathered on April 9, 1865, to end the fighting in Virginia (in other theaters of operations the fighting continued into late April). Before heading to the house, Lee said to his staff that he "would rather die a thousand deaths . . . than surrender this morning to Grant." Longstreet was a touch more defiant, saying: "General, unless he offers us honorable terms, come back and let us fight it out." In another famous exchange over the surrender, Lee asked his subordinates what the country would say if he gave up. One of them said: "Damn the country! There IS no country! There has been no country for a year or so! YOU are the country to these men!"

Lee and Grant had known each other slightly in the Mexican War, and exchanged awkward pleasantries, with Grant babbling on until Lee pushed him to move the meeting along, by saying he had come to surrender, not for tea. Lee assumed he would be taken prisoner, but he wasn't. Lincoln had not wanted a "hard peace." Before Appomattox he said to Grant: "Let him down easy. Let him down easy."

The incident remembered from the armistice is that Grant let Southern officers keep their sidearms and horses, for the spring planting season. The confusion arose over the issuing of 30,000 "paroles," pieces of paper authorizing the Confederate troops to travel home without being charged with desertion. Northern printers were hard pressed to find ink, paper, or presses for such a job. A few days later General Joshua Chamberlain, of Gettysburg fame, accepted the surrender of the army from Confederate General John B. Gordon, who said, after Chamberlain's men lined up and saluted the vanquished Confederates, that he was "one of the knightliest soldiers of the Federal Army."[4] Only in his memoirs did

---

4: Another Confederate officer said, however: "You astound us by your honorable and generous conduct. I fear that we should not have done the same to you had the case been reversed."

the eloquent Chamberlain speak of Appomattox as "the passing of the dead."

After the peace was signed between Lee and Grant, the Appomattox homeowner, Wilmer McLean, did a land-office business selling off the furniture in the room. The English historian John Keegan writes in *The American Civil War*: "As soon as Lee left the room, the members of Grant's staff began to bargain with Mr. McLean for mementoes. George Custer paid twenty dollars for the table at which Lee had sat; Grant's table fetched forty. By the time the party left, the room was bare of furniture." The fate of the McLean house was similarly commercial. When the rebuilding of Appomattox Court House became a 1930s Depression-era public works project, the house was reduced to a pile of bricks, as a promoter wanted to move the house to Washington and there put it on public display (for a suitable entrance fee). Nothing came of the venture, however, and even the bricks vanished.

No sooner had Grant signed the peace than he was headed for the train station, first to stop in Washington, where he met his wife, and then to see his children, who were living in Burlington, New Jersey (south of Trenton on the Delaware River) in a house Grant had bought for their safety. The general delivered the armistice documents to President Lincoln, whose wife invited General and Mrs. Grant a few nights later to attend a performance at Ford's Theatre. The general begged off, saying how much he wanted to see his children.

A Major Henry Rathbone and his fiancée, Clara Harris, used the Grants' tickets. The Lincoln assassins had wanted to kill Grant also, and that night made an effort on his train to Burlington. Fortunately, the general's car was locked. When

Grant heard that Lincoln had been shot, he returned immediately to Washington, although he never again saw the president alive. Theirs had been a telegraphic partnership, with the president sending Grant encouraging cables ("Hold on with a bull-dog whip and chew and choke as much as possible") and Grant responding with victories more than acceptance of the president's social invitations. (He once blurted out: "Really, Mr. Lincoln, I have had enough of this show business.") Grant did continue an association with the president's son Robert, who had been in Appomattox on his staff for the surrender and then in Washington when his father was shot. By some twist of dark fate, Robert Lincoln was also present when presidents Garfield and McKinley were assassinated, the kind of coincidence that ought to merit the attention of conspiracists.

Patrick Henry's Red Hill:
"I am not a Virginian, but an American"

I WAS NOT IN A RUSH TO LEAVE the Longacre Bed & Breakfast. Over coffee I browsed in the downstairs library and padded around my room, answering emails and studying my maps. I knew I wanted to spend the afternoon in Roanoke, Virginia, about two hours to the east, at the O. Winston Link Center in the Norfolk & Western station, which is now a museum. On the way there I had several options. The Booker T. Washington National Monument, a recreation of his boyhood home and some buildings on the Burroughs farm, was near Roanoke. I have always liked his quote: "I had the feeling that to get into a schoolhouse and study would be about the same as getting into paradise." Also en route was Poplar Forest, a summer home that Thomas Jefferson designed and built (although rarely used). I also had a brochure for the National D-Day Memorial in Bedford, Virginia, although I suspected patronage and admission fees, especially given that Normandy is a long way from Virginia.

By consulting the map over breakfast, however, I decided on Patrick Henry's house at Red Hill, south from

Appomattox. For the longest time I have owned one of his biographies, but had gotten nowhere with the chapters that recall the famous quote of his life: "Give me liberty or give me death." I thought a visit to his estate might make his personality more immediate or at least get me beyond page 35, which is where I found my bookmark when I got home and returned to the biography.

Although it was a beautiful spring morning, I was the only visitor at Red Hill. The director fussed over my arrival, as though perhaps Henry was awaiting me for coffee. She guided me through the small museum and turned on the film strip about his life. I had the feeling I was back in Sunday school and Henry was one of the apostles—although his cause was liberty more than Christianity. I had yet to read *A Son of Thunder: Patrick Henry and the American Republic* by Henry Mayer, but I warmed to this founding father's spirit during the film when he said he stayed away from the 1787 Constitutional Convention in Philadelphia because he "smelled a rat."

Until my visit to Red Hill, and later my reading of the Mayer biography, I had not realized that it is to Henry that we owe the inclusion of the Bill of Rights in the Constitution, without which the United States could well have followed George Washington and John Adams into monarchy or, later, despotism.

In his lifetime Henry had many houses and plantations around Richmond, and Red Hill was only his retirement home, where he spent his last years, somewhat removed from political agitation. Nevertheless, even in retirement he could still be counted on for occasional pronouncements, usually on the subject of individual rights. I toured the simple farmhouse where he lived until he died of stomach cancer in 1797 and glanced into his "law office," a small cottage on the grounds with a map of Tidewater Virginia and a desk with quill pens where presumably he dealt with office matters.

The grace of Red Hill contrasts sharply with the attitude of Congress, which after Henry's death refused to recognize his contributions to the republic. Mayer describes the establishment view that Henry was a difficult character. He writes: "In their minds they could apply to Henry himself the popular sarcastic jibe that an 'Anabaptist Preacher' could be brewed in two days' time by taking 'the Herbs of Hypocrisy and Ambition,' two drams of 'the Spirit of Pride,' 'a Pint of Self-Conceitedness,' and four pounds of 'the roots of Stubbornness and Obstinacy' and blending them in 'the Mortar of Vain-Glory, with the Pestle of Contradiction.'" More soberly, Mayer concludes: "In an age of reason he was emotional; in an era of aristocratic stewardship he voiced the demands of the inarticulate."

Henry's talents were as a speaker—he preferred addressing a crowd to drafting a new law—and he was among the first to state: "I am not a Virginian, but an American." Mayer writes that "no man knew better how to rouse common feeling into action," and he quotes from a letter a Connecticut delegate in Philadelphia wrote to his wife: "[Henry is] the compleatest Speaker I ever heard, but in a Letter I can give You no Idea of the Music of his Voice, or the high wrought, yet Natural elegance of his Stile, & Manner."

The point of Mayer's biography is that while Patrick Henry was trained as a lawyer and a practicing politician, he never lost the will to fight for individual rights, and was among the few Virginians who could be called out whenever someone was needed to buck up the opposition to British rule. Most notably, as an Anti-Federalist, his opposition to the Constitution, unless it included protections of civil liberties, was the needed push for later getting the Bill of Rights passed.

At times, later in his life, Henry feuded with Thomas Jefferson and James Madison. They felt he pandered to the raw emotions of the street and that he wasn't to be trusted in compromise, given his hard positions and sharp elbows. Mayer writes: "[They] considered him a schemer and a demagogue. They deprecated his narrow education and his country manners; they disparaged his character as too grasping, too eager for fame and money, and they found something shameful in the way Henry could mobilize popular passion toward political ends."

Jefferson, in particular, had come of political age worshipping Henry's words in Williamsburg's House of Burgesses, remarking that he "spoke as Homer wrote." Later Jefferson blamed Henry for circulating charges of cowardice against him, after the British, led by Benedict Arnold, invaded Virginia in 1779, and then-Governor Jefferson had to flee before the advancing troops. In turn, Henry didn't share Jefferson's Jacobin flirtations and believed "the French Reign of Terror as the inevitable consequence of 'deism and impiety.'" When a mutual friend tried to arrange a reconciliation meeting between the two pillars of the early American Revolution, neither man showed up.

Despite his prickly personality, Henry's political greatness lay in his urging the colonies in the early 1770s to break their political ties with Britain. He rallied them against "the illusions of hope." He said: "There is no longer any room for hope. If we wish to be free, we must fight!—I repeat it, sir, we must fight! An appeal to arms and to the God of Hosts, is all that is left to us." Nor did he believe "relief could be obtained from the king, who had become 'a Tyrant, a fool, a puppet, & a tool to the ministry.'"

Henry's other enduring legacy was his opposition to the Constitution until it included the Bill of Rights. Mayer writes: "Henry did not want the sovereign independent states—the soul of the Confederation—to be taken over by one general government whose extensive powers—the purse in one hand and the sword in the other—would be used to oppress and ruin the people." Mayer continues:

> Virginia's independent constitution began with a Declaration of Rights to protect the people against the possibility of an oppressive state government. The new national Constitution offered no such protection. The rights of conscience, of trial by jury, of liberty of the press, all the privileges and immunities of the citizen would be in jeopardy, if not lost entirely, in the 'alarming transition.'

Driving from Red Hill toward Roanoke, on back-country roads that had red barns and clapboard houses, I wondered what Henry would make of the United States that now endorses "executive action," rendition, so-called Patriot Acts, broad-scale wiretaps, and the prosecution of whistle blowers for leaking information to the press. My feeling is that he would smell a rat.

Roanoke, Virginia:
"To preserve an entire region and a moment in history"

I GOT TO ROANOKE IN THE MID-AFTERNOON, in time to get to the O. Winston Link Museum before it closed. I knew about it from my friend Simon Winchester, who was the first to describe to me the photographs that Link took of the Norfolk & Western steam trains in the late 1950s, before they vanished in the conversion to diesel. Later I came to recognize Link's pictures on railroad calendars and searched for his work online.

Link's photographs are distinctive because he used hundreds, if not thousands, of flashbulbs to cast bright light onto his subjects, usually steam engines. According to a museum book, "Link could fire up to 60 flash bulbs, providing an instantaneous blaze of light equal to more than 100,000 100-watt light bulbs, using shutter speeds of up to 1/250th of a second, to stop the trains moving at 60 miles an hour." Link said wryly, about his need for so many flashbulbs in his work: "You can't move the sun, and you can't move the tracks, so you have to do something else to better light the engines."

Some of his most famous photographs show children frolicking in a river while overhead, frozen in the flash, a steam locomotive crosses a trestle. Other photographs show trains at the end of quiet village streets, or an older couple, arm in arm in a small town, watching the steam era vanish from their lives. My favorite Link photograph is the nighttime image of the *Birmingham Special* glowing in the dark alongside the small wooden station in Rural Retreat, Virginia, while the conductor signals with his lantern for the train to depart.

All of Link's pictures can be seen as elegies for the steam locomotive and the era that ended when the Norfolk & Western, along with all the other American railroads, pulled the plug on the iron horse. In one of his last arranged photographs, Link captures cars parked at a drive-in movie theater, while the screen image is an airplane. In the far distance there is seen the shrinking figure of a steam locomotive.

Late in his life, Link's last work was devoted to the construction of the museum in the derelict Norfolk & Western station. Link's brother said: "The railroad project let him do what he really wanted to do, and it turned out that what he wanted to do was to preserve an entire region and a moment in history."

I wandered through the Link exhibition and watched the film about his life that was showing in an alcove. Link grew up in Brooklyn, New York, and worked as a commercial photographer. Even though he is now associated with Appalachia, he was always a New York City man. He came to the coal fields of Virginia only in 1955. There he discovered not only working branch lines of steam, but the railroad's plan to phase out the engines, which he was determined to preserve, both in photographs and recordings. He later published these as books and records.

When I was growing up, my father had one of these records—either by Link or someone similar. Side A was "Steam with some diesel," while side B had "Diesel with some steam." It was a family joke that it was the only record he enjoyed. Many winter afternoons, when I was doing homework in my room, I could hear "steam with some diesel" wafting up the stairs, perhaps so that my father could bring the coalfields back into his life.

After the war, my father worked as a sales manager for National Sugar Company. His territory was Appalachia, where his only way of getting around was on the train. Perhaps even better than Link, he knew the stations and connections around West Virginia, Virginia, and Kentucky. Later in his life, when we spent hours at the kitchen table talking about trains, he would weigh the merits of the service on the Norfolk & Western and the Louisville & Nashville, the main lines through Appalachia. When I told him about the picture of the station at Rural Retreat, he said immediately: "Oh, yes, on the line to Abingdon," and he would remember the name of a wholesale grocer in nearby Bristol, "Old Man" Davies, who had bought National's sugar.

O. Winston Link:

The Photographer, His Wife, Her Lover

THE ODDEST PART OF THE LINK STORY IS what happened to some of his prints and negatives as a result of his second marriage. His first wife had died, and in 1983 he remarried, to a younger woman, Conchita Mendoza; Link was 73 and she was 48. After his time with the Norfolk & Western ended in 1960, he had worked in advertising, taken pictures in New York Harbor of ocean liners, and retired to Connecticut. Little by little, his photographs were recognized as works of art and priced accordingly. His first museum exhibition was in 1983. For her part in the enterprise, as their relationship progressed, Conchita worked as Link's unofficial agent and marketing representative, helping to build up his national reputation. Every time they needed a little more money, she would send him down to the basement darkroom to run off a few railroad prints, and together they achieved fame and fortune.

Later, in two criminal trials, Link accused his wife of stealing more than 1,400 prints and negatives of his most important works, although not those taken along the tracks of the Norfolk & Western that are now in the museum. Conchita denied the charges and said she had no idea where the prints were and that, for good measure, her husband was senile and beat her. This prompted Link to say she had kept him as a prisoner in his own basement and spent his hard-earned money on her lover, an asphalt and gravel dealer whom Link had engaged to help fix up a steam engine he had acquired.

Judge Jeanine Pirro (another judge on afternoon TV whom my mother and I watched, and a ratings rival to Judge Judy) prosecuted the case, from her day job as a Westchester County district attorney. Because of the affection the jury formed with the avuncular Link, Conchita was convicted and sentenced to six years in prison. When she got out, she married her lover, Ed Hayes, and the story weirdly resumed, with some of Link's missing photographs being offered for sale on eBay and a cache of his negatives and pictures turning up in a mini-storage unit near Gettysburg. She went back to prison for another three years, forgotten to the world until the South African documentary filmmaker Paul Yule rolled up to her prison and taped her recollections of Link and the case for his superb documentary *The Photographer, His Wife, Her Lover*.

In the museum, I had seen snippets of Yule's earlier film about Link, *Trains That Passed in the Night*, which tells the more familiar story of Link heading off to Appalachia with his flashbulbs and cameras to record the fleeting eras of steam and rural innocence. I had a harder time tracking down a print of Yule's newer film, as Amazon.com didn't have a copy for sale. Nor could I stream it from the Internet. Finally I wrote to Yule, and he kindly mailed me a copy of the film from South Africa, where he was born and where he was teaching some courses on documentary films. I watched his film on my computer, assuming it would tell the story of the heists and the wife's betrayal. The film is much more than a crime-scene investigation, raising important questions about marriage, painful divorces, trust, betrayal, justice, the law, and art, much of which—like Link's photographs of the N&W—end up in smoke.

Yule begins the film by explaining that he played a small part in the drama around the missing Link photographs, as the affair between Conchita and Hayes began when Yule was filming his first documentary about Link in November 1990. Yule and Winston had departed for the coal hollows of Virginia, and in their absence Conchita took up with Hayes, who was later convicted along with her for stealing some of Winston's negatives and prints. The story in the documentary, however, is far from the clear-cut case that was published in the *New York Times* after the lovers went to prison and Link's stash of negatives and prints was removed from mini-storage in Pennsylvania.

Yule carefully interviews the prosecutors in the case as well as Link's trustees and lawyers, who handled this case and later his estate. But the most powerful segments of the film are the narratives of the "wife and her lover," who describe Link as descending into paranoia, often beating his wife. In some published reports of the case, Conchita is described as having locked him in their basement ("a virtual prisoner in his own house"), although in the new film his ex-wife says she barred him from the rest of the house because he had used violence against her. When a photograph of her abuse (taken at the hospital after she called the police) was introduced at the trial, Link's lawyers presented evidence that her battered image was the result of plastic surgery on her eyes. Hayes says that on several occasions he intervened to save Conchita from Winston's abuse ("he started mistreating her"). Nevertheless, the court ignored the humanitarian impulses of a lover trying to get between a cheating spouse and her enraged husband.

In the film, the prosecutors make the convincing legal case that Conchita had taken over Link's financial affairs, depositing checks to his accounts and withdrawing cash from the sales of his photographs. Thanks to Conchita's business acumen, however, Link's photographs no longer sold for $300 in railroad hobby shops, but for $5,000 or $10,000 in prominent New York art galleries, whose bow-tied directors appear in the film to hint that Conchita had locked up Link in his darkroom to spin gold out of old railroad negatives. But the old story of a gold-digging younger woman ensnaring an older, smitten man into marriage and giving away his fortune breaks down in Yule's film sequences from her prison.

Conchita speaks as a spurned and beaten wife who only used the money from his photographs to build them a lake house and who left the marriage with nothing more than the clothes in her closet, while Link kept the house, most of the photographs, the money, and the fame. (She says: "I did something for him that he couldn't do for himself.") On camera she says she took only the things he gave her, although the chances are that when she was throwing her clothes into the trunk of her car, she added in negatives and prints that were at hand—as many aggrieved spouses do with household effects when getting kicked out of a marriage. Not content with a nasty divorce, Link went to the police and denounced her for stealing 1500 of his prints. She says to the camera: "I was disposed of, in a cruel manner." Link's lawyers and estate trustee, however, scoff at her pleas of innocence from behind bars, implying that she was hardly Sleeping Beauty and more like Maleficent preying on an American icon.

Even in the cache at the Pennsylvania mini-storage unit, the "1500 prints" were never found. Conchita is adamant, however, that Link made those prints only in his fervid imagination—that in later years he had turned darkly paranoid and was easily confused by dementia. Link's lawyers say that until the end he remained "sharp as a tack" and that her descriptions of the photographer were part of her elaborate scheme to defraud him. She, however, describes his constant fear that many people he met were trying to "screw" him. He could deal with his prints in a darkroom, but not the outside world, except for a handful of remittance men and lawyers. She says repeatedly that the 1500 prints were never made but that she spent some seven years in jail for having stolen them because— if they had existed—they could have been worth $7 million. Perpetrators of manslaughter, she says, usually serve less time.

Link's son by his first marriage makes several cameos in the film, implying that the wicked stepmother ruined his relationship with his father ("she wanted to own him"), although I suspect the father-son ties were broken long before Link met Conchita. (Link's photographs suggest a degree of authoritarian control that, if extended to his role as a parent, could have made him insufferable.) Walking into court, the son says his father would have been pleased at the verdict sentencing his former wife to years in prison, although to me such a remark—delivered in passing to the camera—confirms much of what Conchita said about Link's heartlessness. I know from many friends that divorces can be contested and bitter, but I have yet to meet anyone who would celebrate his or her former spouse spending six years in prison.

Yule's documentary lasts less than ninety minutes, and he sticks closely to the case narrative of the missing negatives and photographs, cutting back and forth between the lovers and the witnesses for the prosecution. Although Yule's cultivated South African accent can be heard posing questions in some of the film's scenes, he never intrudes on the narrative. Still, his compassion can be seen when he and his camera team are the only ones on hand when Hayes is released from prison and Yule gives him the cash in his pockets.

Hayes appears a broken man at times on screen, but he waits for Conchita while she's in prison and marries her when she gets out. He speaks about her wistfully to the camera, as infatuated with her as he was when they first met in 1990. The prosecutors dismiss his statement that Link gave him some of the pictures that Hayes later tried to sell on eBay, although his story is consistent with his claim that Link was paying him with photo prints for the work Hayes was doing to repair the old steam engine Link had acquired. Hayes speaks calmly throughout the film, even though he was caught at the grade crossing of a marriage running off the rails.

I ended the documentary with a different impression of Link than I had when I opened the diskette and slid it into my computer. In coming to the film, I had seen Link as the myth would have it—as someone who had captured the fading light of the American steam locomotive. I had driven along the tracks of his imagination and lingered in his museum, happy that at least one American railroad had its own photographer-laureate. Those warm feelings left me during the movie.

I began to see Link's pictures less as a celebration of steam locomotives and more as stage sets, artfully arranged, but strangely discordant with their settings. Maybe that is their artistic quality? The photographs are not simply Kodak prints of trains at lonely stations, but hauntingly modern pictures in the way they mix a still life in the foreground with steam in the distance, to make the connection between the interior of the soul and lonesome whistles down the tracks. After watching Yule's film, however, the arrangements of the photographs struck me as manipulative, as though Link's goal was to put each person or engine in its place, to suit his obsessions. I even began wondering if he really liked trains or whether they were just another object he could mold to his desires.

From the film it is hard for me to guess Yule's personal conclusions about the case and those involved. Obviously he has an affinity with Link's professional work, as he has made two movies about his life and career. He describes well the genius of the photographic compositions and their lighting. But the indirect way Yule films Link's estate trustee is in contrast to the direct compassion of the prison interviews with Conchita, and suggests that Yule remains disturbed by the portrait of the artist as someone who dumped his wife and sent her to prison. In the interviews, Conchita comes across as yet another object in Link's photographic life that was arranged for his lightbulbs and then pulled from service.

Yule ends the film with several interviews with the man who inherited and finally fixed up the steam engine Link had first engaged Hayes to repair—beginning the strange set of affairs around the purloined pictures. (Nothing came of the restoration project the first time around, except all the unhappiness.) A steam locomotive buff, the man had called Link several times to inquire about buying the engine that was rusting in the weeds. On several occasions, after the man made his pitch, Link abruptly hung up the phone.

After Link died, the man discovered that the engine had been left to him in the will, an odd gesture for someone so rude in person, but perhaps another glimpse at how Link did business. Dutifully the man and his circle of railroad buffs brought the steam engine back to life, at least on the surface. It is shown in the film's last scenes beautifully restored, although the man confesses that the engine is hollow, as the boilers have been removed. The engine is displayed forlornly in a fenced pen on grass—something to be admired from afar, as if in another of Link's staged photographs. Yule himself supplies the film's last lines, when he says to the steam locomotive man: "But it's on a track . . . going nowhere?"

Abingdon, Virginia:

Under the stars in springtime Virginia

LEAVING THE LINK MUSEUM, I bought railroad souvenirs in the gift shop and wandered around the Norfolk & Western exhibits at the station. A preserved departure board shows where passenger trains once headed from Roanoke, and I warmed to their names—*Birmingham Special, Pelican, Cavalier, Pocahontas,* and *Powhatan Arrow.* I was sure my father had stared at precisely this departure board many times on his trips to Roanoke, where he would stay nearby at the Hotel Roanoke, the N&W monolith that is now a conference center. I walked to a restored part of Roanoke to eat a meal that would make do for lunch and dinner. I still hadn't decided on where to stay the night. Because the weather was glorious, my idea was to drive to the Blue Ridge Parkway and find one of the campgrounds that line the road as it snakes its way along the crests. But by the time I had shopped in a grocery store and gotten my bearings out of Roanoke, the highway that doubles as a national park was closed. With defeat in my heart and the sun beginning to set, I pointed the car toward Abingdon, sad that I wasn't on a night train to Birmingham or Chicago.

Cruising along Interstate 81 in the early evening, I passed an exit for Blacksburg, where Virginia Tech is located and where in 2007 a senior, Seung-hui Cho, opened fire on several classes, killing 32 people and wounding 17 others. Those memories had no appeal, nor did Blacksburg. I carried on, although I found few exits and even fewer motels open for business. Finally, with the sun setting, I spotted a sign for Claytor Lake State Park and decided to camp there for the night. I had my tent, sleeping pad and bag, and enough food for breakfast in the morning. The weather was favorable.

I found the park, paid money at the entrance, and drove around until I found the campsites near the shore of the lake. A few other campers were in the area, but they were parked in large caravans, which have the appearance of a family vacation taken on the Pittsburgh Steelers team bus. My Home Depot tent looked like a squatter's shack compared to these rolling palaces, from which I could see the reflected haze of nighttime television and hear tracks of country music. I set up my tent, brushed my teeth, and read a Civil War history with my camping headlamp, happy to be under the stars in springtime Virginia.

Lying on the hard ground, but with my L.L. Bean (meaning expensive) camping pad, I had some immediate doubts about spending an entire night between what felt like a rock and a hard place. I was thrilled not to be in an interstate motel, even though I was drifting to sleep to the tranquil sounds of a nearby RV's generator. Well before sunrise, however, I made several startling discoveries. One was that the L.L. Bean camping pad had been a ripoff. Had the Bean corporation saved money by lining the mat with stones, roots, or gravel? I wondered, as many were lodged in my back. Second, I had made a grave error when packing only a summer sleeping bag, thinking I would be camping in the warm Appalachian springtime. My bag offered no more warmth than did my summer pajamas. At 3:40 a.m. I was freezing, if not to death, at least to the point of deciding to get into the rental car. The back seat, however, was too short for my frame, and the front seats reclined less than those I had last tilted in high school.

Having sneered at the RV's generator, I couldn't very well turn on the engine to heat the car, so I settled on opening my suitcase and dressing in layers of assorted bicycle clothing. When I woke up around 6 a.m, I felt like the Michelin tire man on vacation. The RV families had yet to stir, nor did any ranger question why I stood in the hot camp shower for fifteen minutes. I was brooding about where I might upgrade my camping equipment. The answer was Walmart, where the next morning I bought a portable cot, winter sleeping bag, and pillow, after which sleeping under the stars became a delight.

I decided to hold off on breakfast until I had logged some interstate miles. There would not be any traffic, and maybe I would find a diner serving eggs with grits. I found exactly that at Joey's Country Kitchen in Rural Retreat, which was on a corner opposite the Link railroad station. I had juice, eggs, biscuits, and coffee—the plate's given name on the menu was Roger—and read the Roanoke newspaper, which had more coverage about the tornadoes on Saturday. Across sixteen states, one hundred seventy-eight tornadoes had killed thirty-eight people and caused damage estimated in the billions. Mercifully, my only problem overnight had been rocky soil and cold, not deadly winds or rain.

Across the street from Joey's I walked around the same station that is in Link's photographs of Rural Retreat. The paint was peeling, and the station looked forlorn, but it was in one piece, and had not been altered since the 1950s. No plaque or other marker noted that the station figured in some of Link's most famous pictures, and it saddened me that only a few freight trains passed through here each day. Where I live in Europe, towns the size of Rural Retreat nearly all have passenger rail service.

The track was in good repair, and the station could easily receive passengers. My utopian dreams were not going to persuade Amtrak to introduce direct service to Abingdon. I did, however, have the idea to write to my college friend Paula Johnson at the Smithsonian Institution's American History branch, to urge her to add the station to the list of historic buildings threatened with destruction. I added some urgency to the letter when I later heard that an investor owned the station and planned to tear it down. Only a year later did I learn that a Rural Retreat Depot Foundation had been formed to save and restore the station, so that its fate would not match that of the steam locomotives Link had captured along its platform. My hope now is that they add a plaque with his words, "I was one man and I tackled a big railroad. I did the best I could."

Saltville, Virginia:
"20,000 years of unbroken history all connected by salt"

From Rural Retreat, I wanted to drive along the tracks, so to speak, and see what had happened to some of the other stations that appear in Link's photography. I took state Highway 11, a two-lane road with many trucks, but it also cut through lovely farmland and enticed me with a sign for the Museum of the Middle Appalachians. A sucker for any detour (the reason my interstate-loving wife is impatient with my meandering travels), I turned off the highway at Chilhowie and followed signs to Saltville, where the museum is located. It was still early in the morning, but the doors were open, and the manager of the museum, Harry Haynes, was there to greet me as if I had traveled all the way from Switzerland to see his display cabinets.

Little did I know, when entering the museum, that I would be there for almost two hours and that Saltville had many times been at the center of the world. The museum starts the Saltville story in the Ice Age and continues through the arrival of Native Americans and the evolution of the town in the context of its salt mines, which put it in play in several Civil War battles. (The early cabinets have many rocks and animal skins.) Later Saltville became a company town in the nascent chemical industry, all of which brought the town fame and fortune. Now, typical of the American economy in the 21st century, the mines and the chemical plants are gone, and in their places are drugstores, vacant lots, and unemployment.

Haynes walked me around the museum, telling me the story of Saltville as though it were the story of humankind. Around the year 1000, Native Americans living in the area grew rich on salt, as can be seen in their lavish beads. When he was operating in the area, Daniel Boone had passed near Saltville. In the Revolution, the British military had derided the population around Saltville as the "men over the mountains."

During the 1770s, two of Patrick Henry's sisters migrated to Saltville with their husbands and families, and they grew rich on the salt trade. Their husbands fought in the Revolution, helping to take King's Mountain in South Carolina from the British. During the Civil War, Saltville's production of salt helped keep the Confederacy in business, and each of the Southern states mined the area for salt that was used with foodstuffs, animals, gunpowder, and in the tanning of leather. In October 1864, an attack from Union forces numbering some 5,000 was driven off, and the next day Confederate troops massacred some of the black American soldiers who had fought with the Union army. Later a trial convicted several CSA soldiers of murder. The massacre, rarely remembered, is among the first involving white Southerners and former slaves.

Modern Saltville took shape in 1892 when the Mathieson Alkali Company (later it was the Olin-Mathieson Chemical Corporation) set up operations to exploit the area, making it among the first chemical plants to operate in the United States. Salt production evolved into the production of alkali products, which were soda ash, baking soda, caustic soda, and alkaline commodities. A local history of Saltville by William Kent, which Haynes quoted from and later gave me, has a chapter called "Romance of Baking Soda," stating: "Finally, Baking Soda made its appearance and was found to be the long-sought source of the gas which could be conveniently and safely handled, and stored on the kitchen shelf."

According to Haynes, in the 1960s a U.S. Air Force production facility around Saltville produced some of the rocket fuel that propelled Neil Armstrong to the moon. Only in 1972 did Olin Chemical cease operations in the area, and the population that had once been more than 10,000 drifted down to less than 2,500, which is what it is today. Haynes described the passage with regret, as it ended "20,000 years of unbroken history all connected by salt."

Grateful for all his Saltville information, not to mention Kent's history, I bought souvenirs from Haynes's gift shop and thanked him for his time. As I was leaving, he was telling me that Thomas Jefferson believed that the "road to freedom leads from King's Mountain (liberated by Saltville men) to Yorktown," and he was on to another story about "the most beautiful spot on the face of the earth," when I had to interrupt to ask for directions to Pound Gap, on the Kentucky border.

Walking me to the car, he told a final tale about the tavern in Abingdon, which dated to the time of Daniel Boone, and how Boone had once or twice "crossed the threshold" of a bar that is still in business. I had to go to a local drugstore to buy batteries (another byproduct of salt?) for my camera, and I stopped on the way out of town to see the remains of the chemical works, which are now overgrown with weeds. The works had survived the Civil War, the Great Depression and World War II, but not the shifting of American jobs offshore.

Dante, Virginia:
Circles of poverty

I WAS HEADED TOWARD WHITESBURG, Kentucky, just across the Cumberland Mountains, but wanted to see some of the coal hollows of the seven counties in southwest Virginia. On a railroad map in Roanoke, I had noticed a short line that went northwest from the Clinch River to Dante, McClure, and Fremont, and I settled on Route 63, which weaves its way from Russell County to Dickenson County along streams that I sensed had long ago been clogged with coal.

Although the day was one of bright spring sunshine, once I headed north on 63, from St. Paul, the valley narrowed and the shades of the coal industry began to cloud the skies. At Dante, I steered the car toward what I could determine was the center of the town, although it was just a guess, as the coal mining community is more a long string of houses and trailers than a village center.

If Saltville had come out of the industrial age with a few drugstores and a new high school, Dante looked as if three shifts were still answering the whistles of the Clinchfield Coal Company, even though it shut down its mines there in 1959. The local museum was closed, although I sensed that some effort was being made to preserve the area's history, which rose and fell on the cuts made into the valley walls that held the deep seams of the American coal industry. For the only time on the trip, I felt like a self-conscious outsider, gawking at Dante's circles of poverty. I thought about lunch in the town, but none of the diners felt right for a European in a rented car with a Walmart camp cot, and I drove on up the road until I emerged from the coalfields and crossed over the Cumberland divide at Pound.

At a rest stop off the highway between Virginia and Kentucky, I found a small memorial and picnic area that recalled the Civil War battle of Pound Gap and some of the Kentuckians who had achieved prominence on both sides of the conflict. Kentucky was the swing state in the war, half free and half slave. Lincoln confessed: "I think to lose Kentucky is nearly the same as to lose the whole game. Kentucky gone, we can not hold Missouri, nor, as I think, Maryland. These all against us, and the job on our hands is too large for us. We would as well consent to separation at once, including the surrender of this capital."

At Pound Gap in March 1862, General James A. Garfield (later president, and assassinated in 1881), one of the youngest Union generals, had pushed the Confederates out of Kentucky and back into Virginia, much to the pleasure of the Republican party, which for the next twenty years celebrated Garfield for his shrewdness and good nature. (In the Civil War it was suggested that he accepted any assignment that would put him in the limelight that might later glow on a political career.) As a party man, he played a large hand in tilting the election to Rutherford B. Hayes in 1876, but found himself opposing Grant's bid for a third term in 1880. Grant treated Garfield with peevish contempt for not stepping aside and letting him run again, although after the wounded president died in Elberon, New Jersey (near Long Branch), in late summer 1881, Grant was the first person to console his widow. For obvious reasons, she was cold to his sympathies.

Whitesburg, Kentucky:
The Kennedys come to Appalachia

MY REASON FOR HEADING TO WHITESBURG, Kentucky, was
to visit the home town of the writer Harry M. Caudill, whose
book *Night Comes to the Cumberlands*, about coal mining and
Appalachia in the 1960s, had first gotten me interested in the
area. My father bought the book when it was published in 1963.
I read it as a senior in high school, while doing an independent
study course on the coal mining industry. Caudill was a lawyer,
legislator, educator, and writer, who published a series of books
in the 1960s and '70s about the coal industry. *Night Comes
to the Cumberlands* drew the attentions of John and Robert
Kennedy, who both campaigned in West Virginia around the
themes of neglect of coal miners and their communities. In
1968, before his own run for the presidency was declared, Robert Kennedy had come to Whitesburg to hold Senate hearings
on poverty and to meet Caudill, a local practicing attorney.

Before leaving on this trip, all I had done to prepare for
my stop in Whitesburg was to toss a copy of *Night Comes to
the Cumberlands* into the car. I had no idea whether Caudill's
name was still connected with the county seat. Later, trolling
on the Internet, I found out that the public library in Whites-

burg was named in honor of Harry Caudill, and I decided that would be the place to start my search into his life.

The library is on the main street of Whitesburg, which is a county seat, and thus more prosperous than other towns in the area, but still on the faded side of its glory years. I had to ask directions before I found the library. After parking near the courthouse, I came across a marker indicating that the U-2 pilot Gary Powers (shot down over Russia in the Cold War) was from a nearby community. While shops lined the main street, not all the buildings were occupied, suggesting that coal was no longer king in eastern Kentucky.

The library reminded me of the one I used in Port Washington, New York, when I was growing up and had to pull together a term paper on either elephants or Mexican independence. The card catalogues, still in use, were near the front door, as was a statue of Harry and Anne Caudill and their portrait. All around were school children, perhaps at work on their own elephant term papers, and the open shelves of the collection. A children's section was in one corner, where mothers were trying to corral toddlers. At the reference desk I explained that I was looking for information about Harry Caudill and wondered if perhaps someone at the library had known him.

After some discussion behind the desk, the head librarian, Patty Hawkins, introduced herself and invited me to her office. She had never met Harry, but knew his widow, Anne, and said how pleased she was that I had come from Switzerland to look into the life of Caudill. After talking in the office, Hawkins walked me around the library, showing me a collection of articles the library had saved about Caudill's life, as well as a shelf of his books. She described how Robert Kennedy had come to the library when he stopped in Whitesburg in February 1968 (how many presidential aspirants now stop at public libraries?) and autographed a book.

When I asked if I could see his signature, I expected to be led to a locked rare-book collection, but the book, *The Heir Apparent: Robert Kennedy and the Struggle for Power* by William V. Shannon of the *New York Times*, was on the circulating shelves, filed in Biography under the letter K. Robert Kennedy had signed his name in black ink and wrote the date, February 14, 1968. Under the signature the library had pasted a "Due Date" card and noted the book was not to be taken out of the building. Hawkins said that an event recreating the visit of Robert Kennedy in February 1968 to the coal counties had been staged in 2004, and that over four days Whitesburg had relived the excitement it had not known since Robert Kennedy came through town with his motorcade, pictures of which were in the library's collection. They showed Kennedy sitting on the back seat of an open convertible while the motorcade made its way through hollows that looked a lot like Dante's vision of hell.

While we sat in her office, Hawkins gave me Anne Caudill's address near Louisville and a phone number, and encouraged me to get in touch, saying that she enjoyed talking about her husband's life and work. When I was done with my travels, Anne and I exchanged letters and phone calls. A few months later I arranged a phone interview that her son James helped to set up. Although she was almost ninety years old, Anne's voice and memory were clear and sparkling. We talked for more than hour as she went through Harry's life and work, of which she was a vital ingredient.

Harry M. Caudill Takes On Big Coal:
"It made him angry"

HARRY GREW UP IN WHITESBURG and attended the local schools through high school. Anne told the story of Harry's father, who had lost an arm in a wood mill accident in 1917, before he had children. He had an eighth-grade education and had gone to work to help his mother, after his own father died. Harry's father had an active mind, serving as county clerk, which led him into coal politics and the Letcher County Democratic party. He needed someone to drive him to the meetings. An older brother of Harry's had driven their father early on, but when that brother died, another sibling took over the car. Finally Harry became his father's driver. For a number of years they criss-crossed Appalachia, even venturing as far as the state legislature in Frankfort. The drives gave Harry his early political education. He got to know politicians and miners, heard their stories, and went to their houses and the mines.

Anne and Harry met after the war when she was working as an organizer of agricultural clubs and groups such as 4-H. He was working toward a law degree at the University of Kentucky. When their children were no longer infants, she wanted to "get back into the workforce" and took a shorthand course so she could help her husband around his law office. That led to a collaboration on all kinds of projects: political, literary, and social. He would write on yellow legal pads or dictate to her, and she would transcribe his manuscripts and letters on a manual typewriter. He could not type, except by hunt and peck. "He didn't make notes," she remembered. "He didn't consider he was doing research. He was just dictating to me what he heard."

In the 1956 presidential election, Harry served as the Letcher County campaign chairman for Adlai Stevenson, but got nowhere with the miners, many of whom had served under General Eisenhower in WW II. Harry gave a speech for Stevenson before the Veterans of Foreign Wars, but Anne said the talk "went flat," something Harry found frustrating. Harry had served in the army in the campaigns in North Africa and Italy, and in that service had seen ghost villages on mountaintops and denuded forests, especially along the spine of Italy. He came back to Appalachia to find the same conditions in his home counties. "That made him angry," Anne said, "especially about strip mining, and its successor, mountaintop removal." It's one of the reasons he supported Stevenson, but the veterans voted for Ike.

Harry served three terms in the legislature, his last one ending around 1960. As Anne put it: "He knew that if he stayed in office he would not be able to speak his mind." About that time, an anonymous article "by a Kentucky legislator" appeared in *Harper's Magazine* under the title: "How an Election was Bought and Sold." It begins: "Last year I was elected to the Kentucky legislature after paying off many of the citizens in my district with the money and whiskey they demanded in return for their votes. Many of the men who sit with me as legislators were elected in the same way." In the state capitol, it was assumed Harry had written the article, as few legislators could write for a national magazine. Not all of his colleagues appreciated his revelations about the state House being "an orgy of money grabbing."

After serving in the legislature, Harry got into the habit of dictating to Anne the stories he heard in the office, at political meetings, and around the coal hollows. From these stories, which she typed triple-spaced on long legal sheets of paper, grew a stack of manuscript pages almost a foot high. In 1962, Anne's friend Mary Bingham came to visit in Whitesburg and asked if she could look at the manuscript. She stayed up late at night reading it, and then took it back to Louisville, where her husband's family owned and edited the *Courier-Journal.*

Mary thought the manuscript should be published, and asked if she could send it to her son-in-law, Whitney Ellsworth, an editor at the Atlantic Monthly Press, then part of Little, Brown. He accepted the book for publication, provided the foot-high stack of manuscript pages was culled. Anne and Harry (together with her old manual typewriter) went up to a friend's house in Vermont. For two weeks they hacked at the manuscript. From that effort came the finished draft of *Night Comes to the Cumberlands: A Biography of a Depressed Area,* which came out in 1963.

I asked Anne about Harry's relations with coal mine owners and operators, and she said: "He knew all of them. His father and his brother had been injured in the coalfields. They came from the same background. Many cousins worked in the hollows. He knew the head of U.S. Steel's local coal operations."

After *Night Comes to the Cumberlands* was published, Harry ran into an acquaintance on the street, who said to him that the book had "divided Kentucky in a way that it not been divided since the Civil War." He also said that half the state "wanted him to be the next governor" and "the other half wanted to lynch him." Then the coal man added somewhat apologetically: "What we were doing, no one said we couldn't do it."

Harry never met or spoke with John F. Kennedy about the book, although the president had a copy of Caudill's book and admired it. His secretary of the Interior, Stewart Udall, wrote the foreword. After the book's publication, Harry met many political leaders in Washington and elsewhere, including Lyndon Johnson, Sargent Shriver (whom he encouraged to send VISTA workers to Appalachia, which he did), Senator John Sherman Cooper, Wilbur Cohen (secretary of health, education, and welfare), Senator Gaylord Nelson, and Senator Alben Barkley.

In the White House in December 1964, Harry, along with Representative Carl Perkins from Kentucky, was present when Judge Arthur Dixon presented Lyndon Johnson with a replica of Old Betsy, the rifle Daniel Boone carried across the Cumberland Gap. Judge Dixon had made it by hand, and Johnson treasured the gift. Years later, at the University of Kentucky, the Caudills met Lady Bird Johnson at a reception after she had given a speech. Caudill introduced himself in the receiving line, and Lady Bird said: "Oh, you're the man who gave my husband that beautiful rifle. There's no gift he ever treasured more. I can't tell you how many times he took it off the wall of his office and showed it to visitors." Johnson supported the work of the Appalachia Regional Commission, carrying on the work of President Kennedy, but he had a more immediate link to the area, as the Johnson clan originally came from Johnson County, Kentucky, between Appalachia and Lexington. Texas was an afterthought.

Anne's memories of the visit from Senator Robert Kennedy in February 1968 were clear and sharp. Kennedy was chairman of a Senate subcommittee on hunger and poverty. He had held earlier hearings around the country—in Mississippi and at the Pine Ridge Reservation in South Dakota. In February 1968 he decided to spend three days in Appalachia, holding hearings and investigating the plight of what Harry had called a "depressed area."

Kennedy landed in Lexington and gave a speech there at the University of Kentucky. He drove slowly to Hazard and gave another speech at Alice Lloyd College, in nearby Pippa Passes. The next day he came to Letcher County and Whitesburg. On the way, Harry Caudill joined the motorcade and directed the senator to some of the strip mines and coal hollows along the route.

In Whitesburg, on February 14, 1968, Kennedy spoke on the courthouse steps. When he stepped out of his car, as Anne recalls, a swarm of teenagers engulfed him. She said: "My, that was a revelation to me, to see all those teenagers around him." The procession continued to the town of Neon, once a small trading center, where in a shabby school gymnasium, the Senate subcommittee, under the chairmanship of Robert Kennedy, set up its hearings and called as a witness the CEO of U.S. Steel's local coal mining operations. Harry also gave testimony. He told Anne that he was impressed with the professionalism and empathy with which Kennedy conducted the questioning. "Well," she said, "he was trained as a lawyer, for sure, but my husband very much admired how he handled himself and the witnesses. Very kind. Very sharp. "

After the hearings, Kennedy was driven to a small landing strip somewhere in the hills to take a short flight back to Lexington and then to Washington. He was traveling with his staffer Peter Edelman, and Harry went with them to the airport. As Kennedy was walking to his plane, he stopped, turned around, and walked up to Harry. He grasped his hand and said: "Mr. Caudill, we're going to do something about all this." Four months later Robert Kennedy was dead, and with him went the national concern for the fate of Appalachia.

* * *

HARRY RETIRED FROM THE LAW at the end of 1975. There was a party for him. Toward the end of his legal career, he had hired a partner in hope that the workload might diminish. Instead it "only doubled the number of people who would come to the office." After retiring, friends would ask him, "What do you plan to do now?" He would say: "Oh, just stare vacantly out the window." According to Anne, he did "a little of this, a little of that" and "read a lot," but then their friends at the University of Kentucky, Otis Singletary and John Stevenson (later president of Berea College), came to Whitesburg for a long weekend. Harry had promised to take Dr. Singletary, president of the University of Kentucky, on what he called "the grand tour" of the coalfields, and the weekend selected was in spring 1976. As it happened, Anne's friend Mary Bingham (who had had a hand in publishing *Night Comes to the Cumberlands*) had called to say that she and her daughter, back from college, also wanted to come out that weekend. Fortunately, Anne's older children, James and Diana, were away at school or working, and her younger son was shipped off to friends, giving the Caudills enough bed space for their many guests.

During the weekend, Dr. Singletary broached with Anne the question of whether Harry might like to teach at the University of Kentucky. She said, "Well, he's a born teacher," but begged the president not to mention to Harry that he had spoken with her about a possible position. After the weekend, Harry received a call, offering him not just a part-time position but a full tenured professorship. He said, "Well, I will try it for a semester, and if I don't like it, I'm coming back." He stayed eight years at the university, from August 1976 to May 1984. In the meantime, he and Anne spent weekends and summers at their house in Whitesburg, which they built in 1949 and left only after forty-two years.

At the end of his life, Harry was plagued with Parkinson's disease, and the doctors had told Anne that often a patient's thoughts can turn to what she called "a dark end." His legs no longer supported him, and he was in constant pain. In 1990, just after they had closed on the sale of the Whitesburg house to a young couple, he went back to the home he loved and shot himself in the head with a .38 pistol he owned.

Anne moved to a suburb of Louisville to be closer to her grandchildren and to work on Harry's papers. The original manuscripts for "Cumberlands" and other Caudill books are at the library of Berea College. Otherwise, the Caudill papers are collected at the University of Kentucky, which she said has an index online. Anne said it covers one hundred five boxes, as he wrote ten books and some one hundred sixty two articles, including the hot potato published in *Harper's*. He gave more than one hundred thirty lectures. At least those are the lectures Anne noted down, after 1978, when he was in great demand as a speaker.

She explained that the first library in Whitesburg, in the late 1950s, was in a Quonset hut left over from the war, where the state and local volunteers collected what few books they could find. The Caudills helped push through a small tax that supported the creation of a local library, and that subsidy allowed Anne and others to develop a bookmobile and other library services. In 1994, the new Caudill Library was dedicated on the main street of Whitesburg. She said: "His life was not one with hard edges, so his careers as a lawyer, writer, speaker, legislator, and teacher all blurred together."

Kingdom Come State Park, Kentucky:
Joyriders and bears

BECAUSE IT WAS LATE AFTERNOON when I finished at the library, I decided on an early dinner in the Courthouse Café, which I had spotted when parking the car and thought looked attractive. I ordered one of the homemade dinners from the menu, and immediately fell into conversation with the man on my right, Paul Nesbit, who had read Harry's book "three times," and the café's owner, Josephine Richardson, who had known Harry well. She described the time on a hot summer day when he had grown tired of his work, sought her out, and said, "Come on, let's go swimming." She said he was like that: "spontaneous, warm, and a friend to many."

Josephine studied at Yale and came to Appalachia in 1969, after the well-publicized visit of Robert Kennedy, and had known Harry for the rest of his life. Her husband was an architect and she ran the café, which displayed paintings from local artists. She told me about the local production that had been put together around the Kennedy hearings. She also encouraged me to see a film that Robert Kennedy's son, of the same name, was producing about the devastating effects of mountaintop removal and strip mining. She didn't think *The Last Mountain* was out yet, but knew it would be released shortly. The mountains that had been stripped open like the top of a soft-boiled egg were all around, she said, and she talked about how mining companies found it cheaper and more expedient to dump the sludge and rocks from their excavations into nearby streams, and forfeit their cash bonds, than to restore the land as the law required.

I drove out of Whitesburg in the early evening, followed the directions I had been given, and went past the house where the Caudills had spent their adult lives. There were cars parked in the driveway, and the house had a large deck off the front. I saw no reason to ring the doorbell, although I took a picture, which I am sure the neighbors who were watching me thought suspicious. I turned the car around and headed toward Harlan County on a back road that followed a stream lined with dogwoods. Here and there I passed small wooden houses framed with traditional front porches, which reminded me of the photographs Walker Evans had taken in the South during the Depression.

My idea for the night was to camp in Kingdom Come State Park, which I found up a steep drive off Route 119. The park's name comes from the evocative local novels of John Fox Jr., including *The Little Shepherd of Kingdom Come* and another, *A Knight of the Cumberland*, which Harry had altered when picking a title for his own book. No rangers were stationed in the office, and I drove up and down the park roads, wondering if I could camp and where to pay. Clearly, I was the only camper in the park, although when I finally came across a ranger he told me where to pitch my tent (not to mention my cot, winter sleeping bag, and pillow). It felt a little creepy to be in a Kentucky state park with night approaching and no other campers in sight. I made the best of it and snacked from my cooler while writing notes from the day. I even set up a picnic table as my field desk, with my maps opened and my books arranged for what looked like a seminar on either Appalachia or the Civil War.

Closer to dusk, another camping group arrived—two men and a woman from Chicago. They had a pickup truck, a huge, elaborate tent, things to grill, and firewood, which they shared with me. They had been at the park the night before and said they were down from Illinois to drive the Appalachian back roads in their truck. They confirmed that the park at night attracted not just local joyriders, who would cruise the park roads, but bears, neither of whom sounded like enticing company. I had one of their beers and heard about their off-road drives. They were stunned at the damage being done by the mining companies. Nor did they think much of the locals, who found it suspicious that a pickup truck with Illinois plates was on so many back roads. They were happy to be heading home in the morning.

After a while the conversation switched from strip mining to other tales from the road. I thanked them for the beer and the firewood and went back to my tent to lock the food in my car and prepare for the night. Even though one end of my cot stuck out of the small tent (would it tempt the bears?), the new bed made sleeping a delight. I read for a while by my campfire and drifted to sleep, wondering if the stick I had dragged into the tent would do much if one of the bears decided to try out either the new cot or my winter sleeping bag.

Lynch, Kentucky:
A pickaxe and a wheelbarrow

NEITHER BEARS NOR JOYRIDERS interrupted my night, and I left the next morning for Benham, which has a coal mining museum, and Portal 31, where one of the old mines is open for tourists. I had thought I would start in the museum and move on to Portal 31. The director of the museum said a group was going into the mine and if I wanted to see it I should join them. She even called the office at Portal 31 to add me to the group. When I got down the road to Lynch, it seemed as though everyone was expecting me and knew my name. Later, on the phone with my wife, I joked that I now had more friends in Harlan County than I did in Switzerland.

The tour of the mine was not starting immediately, so I walked around the Louisville & Nashville station in Lynch, which has been restored (although no trains come through) and is part of the Coal Heritage Trail. Even now, the story of many American railroads is the history of hauling coal from places like Lynch to the industrial centers, or now to foreign markets. Railroads like the Pennsylvania, the Chesapeake & Ohio, the Louisville & Nashville, and the Norfolk & Western all had profitable coal transport divisions, and the pictures

Winston Link took in Rural Retreat and Abingdon could easily have been taken in Benham or Lynch.

The biggest problem for the railways on this side of the Cumberland Mountains is the coal needs to move either north or south before it can find a gap and travel East to places such as New York or Baltimore. Many of the recent large mergers of freight railroads, such as that between the Norfolk and the Southern, can be understood as attempts by the railroads to rationalize and expand their coal business—at a time when U.S. consumption is down, due to environmental regulations, and foreign usage is up, thanks to all those coal-burning plants in China. One reason Warren Buffett invested $32 billion to privatize the Burlington Northern Santa Fe Railroad was to haul containers of merchandise from China to Walmart and, on the return, American coal to the Far East.

With a group of Mennonite families, I waited to go into the mine at Portal 31. The younger children were running about, and their parents were encouraging them to mind their manners and stay out of the road. None in the group of about twenty-five would even make eye contact with me, let alone strike up a conversation. To them I was invisible, and I was surprised no one objected when I was the only adult put on the coal conveyor train with a group of boisterous Mennonite children. Maybe, like all parents, they were grateful for a little quiet time.

Hokey as the mine tour was—the cars stopped in front of mechanical miners as if Disney had scripted the descent, and one miner had with him a canary in a cage—I was pleased to see the inside of a mine seam and get a better appreciation of the way mining started as a venture with a pickaxe and a wheelbarrow and turned into an industry that, to increase profits, slices the crests off nearby mountains. In my notebook, I wrote down the inscription on one of the plaques: "These portals were finished in 1920 while coal was being removed from temporary portals to the west. The main haulage went straight through the mountain to Lewis Creek in Letcher Co., while an offset continues to Colliers Creek, about five miles away. The mine was closed in 1963. In 1968, the three main entries were rehabilitated to serve the new Winifrede mine borehole, 1800 feet underground. The conveyor here hauled coal at 500 tons per hour from the Winifrede mine to a 2300-ton storage silo at the tipple."

I was also happy to be in Lynch, where some of the most violent conflicts took place between coal miners trying to unionize and operators trying to keep the organizers away. Later, when I re-read *Night Comes to the Cumberlands*, the towns and mines I imagined on every page looked a lot like Lynch or Benham.

Night Comes to the Cumberlands:
"It corrupts but never purifies"

CAUDILL BEGINS THE BOOK by describing the nearby Pine and Black mountains—"straight as walls and almost as steep"—and goes on to say that "when the streams carved out the mountains and ridges of today they sliced through magnificent seams of coal, a mineral the steel age would esteem more highly than rubies." Nevertheless, he concludes in the introduction that: "Coal has always cursed the land in which it lies. When men begin to wrest it from the earth it leaves a legacy of foul streams, hideous slag heaps and polluted air. It peopled this transformed land with blind and crippled men and with widows and orphans. It is an extractive industry which takes all away and restores nothing. It mars but never beautifies. It corrupts but never purifies."

In the early years of the 20th century, the coming of the railways into the coal hollows transformed what had been a community of lumbermen selling off pristine native hardwood forests into the furnace pits of the industrial revolution. The tracks snaked along rivers such as the Poor Fork of the Cumberland, the North Fork of the Kentucky, and the Levisa Fork of the Big Sandy. Towns with names like Greasy, Stinking, Hell for Certain, Kingdom Come, Frying Pan, War Branch and Hell Mountain spoke to the conditions of their founding.

Later, as the coalfields became better organized and more corporate, towns were named after the executives of the companies that founded them, hence Jenkins, Dunham, McRoberts, Lynch, and Benham. Caudill continues: ". . . and twenty-five miles away in the shadows of the Big Black Mountain lay Lynch, the biggest coal town of them all, with a thousand buildings and nearly 10,000 inhabitants."

Especially after the boom years of World War I, when coal fueled the Navy and the war effort, the mining companies in towns such as Lynch owned the houses, schools, churches, stores, and, most of all, the lives of the miners. A plaque at Portal 31 notes that in its heyday, Lynch had "six miles of concreted paved streets, fifty miles of water lines, power lines, one of the largest company stores in the world, a hospital, 120-room hotel, bank, post office, elementary and high schools, and 1000 homes served by outhouses connected to a central sewage disposal plant."

According to Caudill, the coal industry never escaped the Depression, which led to high unemployment in Appalachia and increasingly desperate confrontations between management and workers. "Though coal still provided the bulk of the nation's energy needs," he wrote, "its tonnage output had grown far more rapidly than the country as a whole, and had outstripped its market." On President Roosevelt's bank holiday, only three banks were open in the plateau. On that day the companies "ceased to pay wages in currency and the scrip disks became practically the only medium of exchange in many counties. . . . The Great Depression was nowhere more appalling than in the coal counties of the Cumberlands.

There destitution came first and stayed longest. There, for most, destitution still persists." About the dole Caudill concludes: "It continued so long it became a standard ingredient of life, and a generation grew up with it as their constant helpmeet and companion."

Caudill describes the increasingly violent confrontations over union representation: "'Bloody' Harlan County acquired its famous prefix during these years because there the Harlan County Coal Operators Association, marshaled by the United States Coal and Coke Company, fought a violent, years-long campaign to prevent their employees from taking the 'obligation' required of United Mine Workers (UMW)."

Ironically, although they are only a few miles apart, the union battles split the towns of Lynch and Benham. The latter voted for the Progressive Mine Workers, often called "a company union." "Nevertheless," writes Caudill, "its organizers made headway and at one time had pockets of membership in a good many camps. But they were too few to withstand the triumphant forces of John L. Lewis [and the UMW] and after 1934 their organization withered and vanished from the plateau—with the exception of the town of Benham in Harlan County, where Progressives remained in control and became the bargaining agent for the miners. Friction between this union and the huge UMW at nearby Lynch was constant, erupting from time to time in gunfire."

Even as the UMW became triumphant across Appalachia—in the words of John L. Lewis, as quoted by Caudill, he made the operators "come to Carnossa"—post-World War II industry cut back its reliance on coal. Railroads such as the Norfolk & Western retired their steam locomotives, and power plants converted to oil. Caudill says it wasn't all a question of price or supply and demand: "The industry's consumers had patiently borne the burdens piled onto them by their suppliers. Their engineers had wrestled with furnaces choked with unburnable slate, and their purchasing agents had sworn in exasperation over the price gouges with which the producers and brokers afflicted them."

Faced, as Caudill writes, with the "dwindling price of their product and the soaring costs of their labor and supply," coal operators resorted to available technology and turned mining into an open-pit industry, which could be run with dynamite, trucks, scrapers, and conveyor belts instead of miners with lunch pails and canaries. The company towns were shut down (by the 1950s "only Benham and Lynch in Harlan County and Wheelwright in Floyd County retained their towns"), and the mining companies moved from the hollows to the mountaintops, leaving behind most of the miners. ("To this day rows of rotting shacks can be found climbing snakily around brown, eroded hillsides, their walls and roofs sagging beneath a quarter-century of neglect and their vacant windows staring reproachfully at the heedless world.") Caudill laments: "With strip mining and its companion, the auger-mining process, the shades of darkness moved close indeed to the Cumberlands."

Caudill's 1963 book is prescient about the effects that mountaintop removal would have on the area fifty years later. The script of Robert Kennedy Jr.'s 2011 documentary could have been gleaned from Caudill's text. Inadequate mineral-rights laws still make it possible for coal companies to strip the landscape bare, although when he wrote, Caudill observed that the legislation "bestowed upon the owner of a seam of coal the right to destroy totally the surface insofar as any known system of reclamation is concerned." He said: "The evil effects of open-cut mining are fantastically magnified when practiced in the mountains. . . . Such an operation can transform a razorback spur into a flat mesa." He quotes a judge who ruled against one disgruntled land owner who was protesting what was happening on the land he had leased to a mining company: "The truth is that about the only rights you have on your land is to breathe on it and pay the taxes."

With foreboding, Caudill notes that "practically every ridge, spur and point in the eastern Kentucky coalfield is a candidate for strip and/or auger mining." He even quotes one of the miners: "Since then we have gutted these old mountains and shaved 'em off clean. Now we are skinning 'em and cutting their heads off."

I read Caudill's book as more than just a history of Appalachia and coal mining until 1962, although it is certainly that. To me the book feels like a meditation on capitalism, with many open questions about how a nation can both consume its natural resources and return some of the wealth to the area from which it was quarried and removed.

Caudill understands that if miners are paid a livable wage and coal companies are forced to restore the landscape to its original condition, the industry might not be competitive with oil or other forms of energy. Nevertheless, he condemns the cruel irony in the existing system that Appalachia is among the poorest regions of North America while sitting on top of the nation's most abundant resource, which could fuel the United States for hundreds of years.

"The nation," he states, "has siphoned off hundreds of millions of dollars' worth of its resources while returning little of lasting value." I wonder what he would think to hear that the mountains of Appalachia are now being drawn and quartered so the coal can be sent to the furnaces of China.

Caudill's sympathies were with the miners and the land-scape, the tail end of an energy supply chain that cared little for the welfare of either. He saw the miners as the heirs of the Scottish-Irish immigrants (men from "over the mountains") who carved for themselves lives of political and economic autonomy. Mining, governmental dependence, and economic servitude only made the miner suspicious and lax. "Bit by bit," he writes, "his self-reliance and initiative deteriorated into self-pity."

Although the quotation is not in his book, I think Caudill would have agreed with the sentiments of Clarence Darrow, who in 1903 represented the United Mine Workers in Pennsylvania at an arbitration and said: "Five hundred dollars a year is a big price for taking your life and your limbs in your hand and going down into the earth to bring up coal to make somebody else rich." As for the landscape, Caudill writes: "A relatively stable mountain, whose soil and water were to a high degree protected by grass and trees, had been reduced to a colossal rubble heap."

In some of the book's most haunting language, he describes the view from places like my Kingdom Come campsite—"Seen from such eminences the lesser hills and ridges appear as gigantic waves on a primordial ocean." At the same time he knows that one bad side effect of King Coal is that occasionally the mountains catch on fire and burn for months, as happened in the 1920s. He writes: "The fires cast off clouds of oily black smoke which settled in the valleys and enveloped the homes of boss and miner alike, immersing them in a gray dinginess and in nauseous fumes heavy-laden with sulphur."

What Caudill most had in mind was a coal industry that was sustainable for the miner and environment alike, in which the miners would earn a livable wage and the companies would have to respect a landscape that could easily have formed the backbone of a national park or forest, were it not being ripped apart in the search for hydrocarbons.

Throughout the book, Caudill uses the common expression, "I was born with coal dust in my blood," to describe friends, family, schoolmates, and those he meets on chance encounters. Despite the affection he holds for the men of the hollows and the ground they inhabit, he still concludes that "wherever coal has been mined a blight has fallen upon the land and upon the habitations of men."

The Last Mountain:
Robert F. Kennedy Jr. in his father's footsteps

IT TOOK ME A LONG TIME, after the trip, to track down a copy of *The Last Mountain*, the documentary film featuring Robert F. Kennedy Jr., about the fight to stop, at least on Coal River Mountain, strip mining from slicing off the top of the mountain. After Josephine told me about the movie, I wrote to its press officers, hoping to get an advance copy. That correspondence always ended with their telling me I could catch the film in some place such as St. Louis (not exactly close to my home in Europe).

The movie is set in West Virginia around the hollows under Coal River Mountain, and much of the footage shows grassroots opposition to Massey Energy, the coal company that undertakes more mountaintop removal than any other in America. Residents—living in the shadow of the hills that Massey wants to denude in its search for coal—talk on camera about how nearby streams have been filled in with sludge, cancer has spread in their schools and communities, and coal has enriched corporate shareholders while leaving many West Virginia mountains as slag heaps. Footage is shown in which residents coordinate their nonviolent protests against the encroachments of Big Coal; in some cases climbers camp out in trees to keep the company from cutting open a mountaintop. Links are made between strip mining and the pollution of the water table, and the filmmakers fly in small planes over Appalachia, revealing from the air the extent to which billions of gallons of poisonous sludge—far greater than the amounts of oil that fouled the Gulf of Mexico—sit precariously over towns and schools, often a heavy rainstorm away from becoming a Johnstown Flood of toxic waste. Into this combustible political environment comes Robert Kennedy Jr. to take up his father's mantle in Appalachia and to oppose the same oligarchs that excited the passions of Harry Caudill.

Because Kennedy suffers from a rare voice disease, spasmodic dysphonia, which makes him sound like a tremulous old aunt, he is an unusual star for a documentary film, although the name Kennedy and his legal campaigns to clean up American water make him the obvious choice to personalize the Appalachian fight against mountaintop removal. He is shown flying in a small plane above the stripped mines— imagine huge construction sites in the middle of rural mountains—and on camera he is often confronting Massey corporate officers or local coal boosters with a litany of facts and figures about the ravages that the coal industry has left in the region.

Kennedy talks about 40,000 lost jobs (the big companies prefer automation to miners and canaries), 2000 miles of filled-in streams, five hundred mountains ripped open, and, above all, the way the George W. Bush administration allowed lobbyists for Big Coal to fiddle with the language of the Clean Water Act, making it "less illegal" to treat Appalachia as an open coal pit and then walk away from the sludge lakes. He reminds many of those he confronts that Massey racked up 60,000 violations of the Clean Water Act, to the indifference of the local Department of Environmental Protection, which the West Virginia governor (self-described as "a friend of coal") had stocked with corporate shills.

The Dr. Evil in the film is the chief executive officer of Massey Energy, Don Blankenship, now retired, who mobilizes coal workers against the protesters, on the basis that the environmentalists want to "take away their jobs." Kennedy, however, makes the point that the evolution to mountaintop removal was undertaken precisely to counter the strength of the United Mine Workers union and that Massey accuses the opposition of threatening local jobs as a cover for its own assaults on unions and safety procedures.

At company rallies Blankenship is shown preaching the corporate line and despairing over environmentalists (who invariably are depicted as coming from "out-of-state"), while behind the scenes paying himself during his career almost $200 million in salary, stock options, and bonuses. (Miner fringe benefits are still largely confined to black lung disease). Off camera he describes workers as little more than spare parts. ("If the tool is broke, get another," he once said of miners.) In the film there are endless cuts between company spokesmen (for example, calling a flash flood "an act of God") and protesters lying down in the road as large graders rumble along mountaintop roads ("It's a crime against Appalachia").[5]

5: Ironically, Blankenship was convicted and sentenced to federal prison for having violated mine safety laws. In 2017, he was appealing his conviction to the Supreme Court. In 2018, he ran unsuccessfully for the U.S. Senate.

Kennedy's best arguments are economic, as when he makes the point that if the price of coal included all the costs of polluted water, ruined towns, flash floods, and cancerous workers and residents, it would be one of the more expensive forms of American energy ($0.231 per kilowatt-hour). As an alternative, he promotes the cause of alternative energy, outlining how the ridges of Appalachia could be covered with windmills that would protect the landscape and produce abundant energy. The film shows tired Appalachian coal plants in contrast with snappy pictures of windmills billowing alongside New England beaches.

Although this coda to the documentary feels a bit like a public service advertisement ("If we harness the wind, we can harness our future . . ."), Kennedy's enthusiasm for renewable energy has West Virginia activists putting together feasibility studies for the "last mountain" to be covered with windmills. Nevertheless, as the film ends it is assumed that Massey will harness the more traditional energy of cash to maintain their digging on Coal River Mountain. Around the credits are those slightly cloying follow-up notes that describe how Kennedy's presence had a positive impact on the lives of many of those living under the mountain.

In the film, Kennedy never quite develops the affinity that his father had for Appalachia and its people. The son is shown, in Kennedy campaign style, dropping in unexpectedly on small West Virginia homes (one man says: "I never thought I would have a Kennedy in my house") and speaking impromptu at rallies about the dangers of dirty water and air. He looks distinctly more like a legal outsider—a New Yorker heading down to the coalfields to file a few lawsuits—than did his father, even though the senator only passed through

West Virginia and did little more for the region than to publicize its decline. The senator did, however, share with his fourteen-year-old son, shortly before his death, the premise of the coal industry in Appalachia. He tells his son: "They're doing it to break the unions," a motivation that on camera the son attributes to Massey CEO Blankenship—correctly, I would add.

In some of the autobiographical moments on film, Kennedy describes how a highway built through his favorite, backyard Virginia woods turned him into an environmentalist at age nine. He is shown as a small boy giving his uncle, President John F. Kennedy, a newt in a fish bowl and a short lecture on the need to get serious about protecting air and water. To his credit, the president steers the young crusader in the direction of his cabinet officers, including Stewart Udall, who wrote the forward to Harry Caudill's book. Who is to say that the meeting with the nine-year-old boy didn't change the president's own thinking about the environment, although it is also possible that his administration was funding the interstate that cut through his nephew's beloved woods. When Kennedy describes campaign contributions as little more than "legalized bribes," he might well be describing the conduct of the Big Politics that, in earlier days, gave his family their platform on the national stage.

I am not surprised that I never managed to interview Robert Kennedy Jr. In 2012, not only had his former wife died a suicide, but the *New York Post* got its hands on his 2001 private diary in which his many extramarital romantic conquests are recorded as though they were accounting entries, with the number 10 indicating all receivables having been collected. In such a whirlwind I can easily imagine why he would be shy about granting press interviews, even one devoted to the transgressions of Big Coal in Appalachia. Nor do I think in a press interview that I could have explored how his coal work was mixed up with his last fleeting images of his father, who was killed in the same year that he held his hearings in Appalachia.

At the time his father died, Robert Kennedy Jr. would have been fourteen years old, the same age I was in June 1968, when on a humid summer morning I turned on my bedside radio and learned that the New York senator had been shot while on the presidential campaign trail in California. I remember not wanting to go to school that morning and dragging through the day with dread, as it took Kennedy more than twenty-four hours to die. In class we were given bulletin updates from teachers.

That hot June day I also had the recent images of having met Senator Kennedy, who had come to a small gathering on Long Island of the League of Women Voters. My mother, who was on the board, took me out of school to hear him speak. The meeting took place in a Great Neck living room, no doubt with a tea service on the dining room table. I was the only teenage boy in the small circle of "women voters" that day meeting the senator.

After talking about the Vietnam War and other issues of the day, the senator made a point of engaging me personally on my classes, the football team, books I liked, and other common interests. It wasn't a long conversation, but I remember it as heartfelt. His eyes were locked into mine with intensity, compassion, empathy, and humor. (I think his first words were: "How did you manage to get out of school?") He seemed to have remembered what it was like to be in the eighth grade, and I am sure his enduring bonds with Robert Kennedy Jr. conveyed the same qualities. Less than six months later the senator was lying spread-eagled in that pool of blood in the Ambassador Hotel's kitchen. As I carried my books around to classes, I felt bereft for the family—perhaps one reason both of us, forty years later, found our way back to Appalachia.

Benham to Hazard, Kentucky:
RFK in eastern Kentucky

LATER THAT MORNING I was the only visitor at the Benham Coal Mining Museum, which occupies what had been the company store when International Harvester owned and ran the town. Before going in, I drank a coffee on a bench outside, which overlooked the company theater. Even with the nearby mines shut and unemployment high, Benham is attractive, evoking aspects of a small college campus more than a closed company town.

I liked the museum a lot. Although it had its share of mining tools and lumps of coal, most of the exhibits were about the lives and families of the miners. On display was a kitchen taken from a miner's home, parts of a schoolhouse, many lunch pails, and a temporary exhibit on the "coal miner's daughter," Loretta Lynn. (A mannequin with a flowing wig and long white dress is shown singing into a microphone.) I saw first editions of John Fox Jr.'s books, and young African-American school children posing for a picture on what looks like the occasion of their school play.

The museum also treats sympathetically the many immigrants who arrived at New York's Ellis Island and were then put aboard special trains for Benham or Lynch. It covers the horrific mining disasters, such as the explosion on Black Mountain that killed all six Massengill brothers.[6] The museum has an extensive oral history collection, including the words of a Reverend James Hannah, who in 1980 remembered: "Then what coal you loaded, you got paid for it. If you didn't load no coal, you didn't get paid."

For lunch I drove into nearby Cumberland, a forlorn town straddling the river of the same name, and parked the car near the Touch of the Country restaurant, which was serving a homemade lunch in what looked like a neighborhood kitchen. Just after I ordered, an older man came into the restaurant, spotted me, and asked if that was my car (with New Jersey license plates) parked down the street. Without waiting for my answer, he sat down at the table, ordered his own lunch, and asked me "What brings you to Cumberland?" When I explained about my interest in the life and writing of Harry Caudill, he was off explaining his own involvement with the coal industry (lost to me now) and how he "helped out around the museum" in Benham. Our lunches appeared almost instantly. He made short work of his chicken and biscuits before excusing himself to head off to another appointment.

I got a refill on my root beer and cole slaw, and plotted the next leg of the journey toward Lexington, Kentucky. I

6: A newspaper clipping reads: "The explosion apparently was caused by dust filling the passageway. Mining engineers explained that this is the worst time of the year for such a hazard, since the dry atmosphere increases the possibility of the dust filling the passage, where the slightest spark will set it off with the force of dynamite. Another hazard in this instance was that the Zero mine is one of the oldest in this section, with the entries running well over a mile back into the mountain side, thus making it hard to force air back into them."

wanted to see something connected with Abraham Lincoln's cabins (apparently Kentucky has them everywhere) and the Civil War battlefield at Perryville, which had been the pivotal battle in the state.

Lincoln was born near Hodgenville. I had heard that his cabin there looks like it was built by Ikea, so I decided to focus more on Perryville, south of Lexington, and the log cabin of Lincoln's father at the time he married Nancy Hanks. To get there, I sketched out a route that would allow me to retrace the path of Robert Kennedy's motorcade (although in the other direction) and get on the Hal Rogers Parkway in Hazard. Between Cumberland and Hazard, I would take a twisting coal road through places such as Delphia, Slemp, and Viper—names a little less corporate than those of Benham and Lynch.

The drive over the hills to Hazard was among the prettiest on the trip. I did not mind that I was stuck behind a slow-moving truck and often pulled off the road to take a picture of a coal tipple or railroad hopper cars shunting near the river. The sun was directly overhead, giving the hollows a cheerfulness they had lacked around Whitesburg and Lynch.

In driving across the back counties of Kentucky, I recalled that in 2004, organizer John Malpede had engaged numerous towns, schools, officials, and students in what he called "a real-time documentary-style performance by a large community cast." His goal was "to put an historical mirror up to present-moment life in eastern Kentucky." In the end he had called his extravaganza "RFK in EKY" [Robert F. Kennedy in Eastern Kentucky] and the Robert F. Kennedy Performance Project. Over four days, Malpede's own motorcade had logged two hundred miles and put on readings, performances, and seminars about conditions in Appalachia then and now. Malpede even used government transcripts from Kennedy's hearings as what he called "found text," and had actors and community members read from the original sources.

The events dealing with "art and citizenship" included a memory of Steve Cawood, who had been a young Appalachia Volunteer with Kennedy on the original tour, and who described an episode along the road where I was now driving:

> We were goin' up one of those hollers between there and that strip job. We were driving up this holler and there were shacks and junk cars and that typical stuff you find in a holler. As of a sudden Bobby screams, "Stop this car, stop this car." We didn't know whether we'd run over somethin' or what we'd forgotten or what. We got out and he said, "I wanna go over here and meet these people."

I loved the goals that Malpede set for his bandwagons. "RFK in EKY," he said, "is intent on encouraging the practice of citizenship." Nor had he undertaken the venture to sell Kennedy memorabilia or produce a film. Very few video images survive from the events. He simply wanted more people to remember what had been said.

Perryville, Kentucky:
Blue highways to bluegrass

THE DRIVE TO PERRYVILLE TOOK about two hours. On stretches like these, I regretted leaving in such a hurry as to neglect having in the car some books-on-tape. Nor was I passing bookstores that might be selling audio histories of the Civil War. In most places I went, the local radio was awful, a mixture of bad music and angry conversations. Occasionally, between all the "scans" on the dial, I would find a talk show of interest or a baseball game, but mostly I felt like a hostage of Rush Limbaugh, who would be waiting for me in his dungeon whenever I decided to spin the dial on the car radio.

I was also traveling without GPS, another overlooked purchase. I had thought of buying one for the rental car, but I held back, scared that some vixen in a shrill voice, possibly even Australian, might hector me until I followed her directions to the interstate. For the most part I was sticking to what the author William Least Heat-Moon called "blue highways," although I did use the divided highways as a bridge to my next area of interest.

On the long drives, I rarely had any problems following my determined route, even if I was taking a succession of back roads. The difficulties arose when I needed to find a specific place—say, the Perryville battlefield—and the signs were sketchy. Nor did I follow my father's eternal advice in such situations: "Just pull into a filling station and ask the attendant." Instead, I would dig harder into the maps, sure that the answer to my perplexity could be solved on paper. A few times out in the middle of Kentucky, a compass would have helped, or a smartphone, although mine is registered in Europe.

The entrance to the Perryville battlefield wasn't on Highway 150, but off a side road, Route 1920, which I found only on my second try. I was racing, as I wanted to get to the visitor center before it closed. My fear was that it would shut at 5 p.m. I did make it in time to the visitor center, although because Perryville is a state, not a national, battlefield site, the museum did not include one of those park-service relief maps with dots for marching armies, or a video history.

At this point, I confess I knew next to nothing about the Battle of Perryville. I was there because I had read the name in my Civil War guidebook and because one of the goals for the trip had been to better understand the western campaigns of that war. In my original travel daydreams I had wanted to take in the battlefields around Tennessee and Georgia, especially Shiloh, Chickamauga, and Kenesaw Mountain. They were too far to drive to in my allotted time. If I had flown, I could not have taken my bike or my camping gear (nor, for that matter, slept in the freezing cold at Claytor Lake). Instead, Perryville would have to serve as the proxy for the other battles in the west, although, when I blew through the door of the visitor center, it would have helped if I had known when the battle was fought and who were the commanders.

The ranger on duty, together with a woman working the cash register in the gift shop, said that the office would be closing soon, but that I was welcome to stay as long as I chose on the battlefield. They gave me a guide to the walking trails, sold me a replica edition of *Harper's Weekly* from November 1, 1862, and let me look over the books before making it clear that it was past closing time.

Because it was still hot and I had been driving for several hours, I drank water and read from my book in the shade before setting out on the trails. John Keegan's summary in *The American Civil War* is evocative, but still didn't tell me the particulars of the battle. He writes:

> Perryville was an all-too-typical Civil War battle in its lack of decision, despite high casualties on both sides. . . . Casualties at Perryville—4,200 Union and 3,400 Confederate—were certainly high, but neither side seemed shaken. An eyewitness, Major J. Montgomery Wright of Buell's army, describes the strange phenomenon of the acoustic shadow. Riding as a staff officer on a detached mission, he "suddenly turned into a road and therefore before me, within a few hundred yards, the battle of Perryville burst into view, and the roar of the artillery and the continuous rattle of the musketry first broke upon my ear. . . . It was wholly unexpected, and it fixed me with astonishment. It was like tearing away a curtain from the front of a great picture. . . . At one bound my horse carried me from stillness into the uproar of battle. One turn from a lonely bridlepath through the woods brought me face to face with the bloody struggle of thousands of men.

Clearly, the only way to learn more about Perryville was to walk along its trails, which I did for the next several hours, losing myself in its lonely fields, which, as must have been the case in 1862, I found acoustically cut off from the modern world, and lovely in a late afternoon of full sunshine.

The Battle of Perryville:
Neither victory nor defeat

PERRYVILLE IS ONE OF THE FEW Civil War battlefields that can be seen only on foot. No roads cut through the former lines of battle, and the only way to stay on track is to follow a beaten path through the grass.

The battlefield is initially confusing, because the Confederate army attacked more from the north and east, while the Union forces occupied the hills to the west and south. Logically it should have been the other way around, but the Confederates, under General Braxton Bragg, had ranged farther to the north, threatening Louisville, before turning toward the south, where a Union army was in pursuit.

So sure was Bragg that his march through Kentucky would be a successful recruiting trip that he carried with his forces extra uniforms and rifles, for all those undecided Kentuckians who, after seeing the élan of the Confederate army, would enlist on the spot. Not only did Bragg fall short of his enlistment quotas, but in withdrawing to the south he lost track of the Union forces. They only met, largely by chance, because a water shortage in the area brought both armies to the same watering hole, and the shots over the control of that spring turned it into the largest Civil War battle fought in Kentucky.

Not that the Union army, under General Don Carlos Buell, was much better prepared for battle than the Confederates. He remained with the main part of his army over those "acoustical" hills on what is now Highway 150, and, as Keegan describes, he missed the chance to march to the sound of the guns with his 40,000 men. With better staff work, runners, or perhaps GPS, Buell would have confronted a Confederate army of 16,000 with some 58,000 men, and swept Bragg from the field. Instead, only 20,000 Union soldiers fought at Perryville, and they occupied a series of rolling hills that receded to the south and west like waves on a green ocean.

After the chance encounter at the watering hole, the Confederate regiments did what they did best in 1862, which was to deploy the cavalry and fix bayonets for a frontal charge that could have been drawn up by Napoleon at Austerlitz. *Harper's Weekly* includes this eyewitness description of the battle: "We moved up the hill and nestled close in under the guns, many of the Artillerists had been killed and the ground around was slippery with blood, many a poor dark looking powder begrimed Artillery man was laying stretched out upon the ground around us, torn and mutilated, their countenance plainly indicating the awful manner of death."

As I made my counter-clockwise walk around the battlefield, I read plaques and studied formations at places that now bear the names of many of these attacks: Stewart's Advance, Assault on Parson's Ridge, Defense of Parson's Ridge, The Cornfield, Starkweather's Hill, Stewart's Attack, Donelson Persists, Widow Bottom Site, Jones' Crossing, Cleburn's Advance, Stalemate, Widow Gibson Site, Final Union

Line, Mackville-Perryville Road, Wilkerson House Site. It struck me that with the deployment of a few verbs, those names could be arranged into a poem about the futility of so many Civil War battles, especially with words such as "stalemate" and "the cornfield." Even with more than 7,000 casualties in the Battle of Perryville, it would be hard to describe it, for either side, as a victory or defeat.

At the call to battle, Bragg's men had stretched out in long formations and attacked up the first hill into the Union lines, often breaking through or cutting off pockets of Union defenders. Notably, in the early going, the Confederates charged up Starkweather's Hill, which even on a sunset walking tour is something of a climb, and they almost turned the left flank of the Union army. Had they succeeded, the battle might have decisively swung to the Confederates.

Instead, Union forces drew back to the next set of hills— they look like inland ocean swells—leading the southerners to repeat their valiant charges into the next set of Union guns. In this way, the Confederates won most of the skirmishes at Perryville, in a manner that a poet might describe as heroic— horses surging forward, swords catching the afternoon sun, etc.—but they failed to win the battle. The next day Bragg beat a hasty retreat when he learned that Buell was over the last hill with another 40,000 men. By now the Union commanders had turned up their hearing aids.

Spinning around Perryville:
A diplomat in carpet slippers

ONE OF MANY CASUALTIES at Perryville was the Confederate way of war, those daring cavalry charges into emplaced guns. It had ennobled the annals of war, perhaps, but it depleted the South of its best officers and men, with little result or purpose. The battle also dealt a death blow to the Confederacy's foreign policy in London, where Jefferson Davis hoped to gain recognition for his government. I came to appreciate Perryville's importance to Lincoln's foreign policies only when later I read an excellent book by Jay Monahan, *Abraham Lincoln Deals With Foreign Affairs: A Diplomat in Carpet Slippers* (published in 1945 and reissued in paperback in 1997 by Bison Books at the University of Nebraska).

Monahan makes the point that with no experience in international relations, Lincoln was a master at keeping the French and the English governments from recognizing the Confederacy, a juggling act that required victories in the field (which early in the war were rare) and subtle diplomacy (when the president was shuffling around in his carpet slippers). Lincoln chose to defuse the Trent Affair (the seizure of British diplomats on the high seas), ignore Napoleon III's foray into Mexico, and divide the English govern-ment on the question of whether it was morally right to recognize a slave-holding power for commercial reasons. His foreign policy depended on keeping Kentucky out of the Confederacy. Monahan writes:

> Charles Francis Adams [ambassador to the Court of St. James's] had warned Lincoln that nothing would save the North in Europe but emancipation, yet emancipation would cost him Kentucky. . . . If Kentucky was safe then Lincoln might placate Europe.

Monahan describes the president's skill at the diplomatic game: "Lincoln had split Britain class from class, precisely as he and [Secretary of State William] Seward had separated England and France. The Northern cause had become defi-nitely antislavery. The liberals cheered even when Lincoln stopped and confiscated their countrymen's ships."

Whatever the facts on the ground about Southern heroism, the fighting and maneuvering around Perryville saved Kentucky for the Union and allowed Lincoln to put off the question of emancipation until the fall, by which time there was no chance that the Confederates could take back Kentucky.

Perryville was also an early taste of war for men whose careers and legacy would stretch well beyond the Civil War. General Philip Sheridan fought at Perryville, as did Lieu-tenant Arthur McArthur Jr., the father of General Douglas MacArthur (the "a" came later), who was General Simon Bolivar Buckner Jr.'s World War II contemporary. Buckner also had a father who fought at Perryville (as a senior Confederate general). The latter Buckner commanded the invasion of Okinawa and was the highest-ranking American general killed in the war.[7]

When they met in the Pacific war in the 1940s, did the conversations between generals MacArthur and Buckner return to what their fathers had seen on the rolling hills of Perryville? I can find no trace that either commented about the battle, but Charles W. Carr, from the 24th Illinois Volunteer Regiment, said of it: ". . . you cannot imagine the horror of war. No pen nor tongue can begin to tell the misery I have seen." Sam Watkins, who wrote the celebrated Civil War memoir *Co. "Aytch"* recalls: "It was a life to life and death to death grapple."

The Lincoln Homestead State Park is down the road from Perryville, and I expected to find it surrounded with motels, gift shops, and restaurants, all of which were on my mind after I had lingered on the battlefield. Instead, the small park, consisting of several log or planked houses, sits in a glade five miles from the town of Springfield, where Thomas Lincoln, Abe's father, married Nancy Hanks and then brought her back to his cabin. I was expecting LincolnWorld but came across several small, well-made wooden houses and outbuildings that corrected my misimpression that Abraham emerged from a white-trash encampment.

By all accounts, the Lincolns were a poor but locally prominent family, with a proud lineage to the American Revolution and England. Thomas liked both his extended

---

7: Lloyd Graybar writes of Buckner Sr.: "At Perryville, his aide related, bullets kept whizzing by their heads. The aide kept ducking. Finally, Buckner, seated stoically on his horse, turned and said, 'Lyman, don't dodge; it's all over when you hear the noise.'"

family and living on the prairie in his log constructions, which explains why he moved several times around central Kentucky. His marriage to Nancy Hanks was a celebrated social occasion, with merriment, speeches, and, I am sure, hard cider. A picture of Nancy, displayed outside the Lincoln house, bears a strong resemblance to her famous son (as though, in the photograph, he was wearing a dress). She died in 1818—after drinking milk that was contaminated—when the future president was nine years old. At the end she called her two older children to her bedside, according to an inscription in the park, and told them to be "good and kind to their father—to one another and to the world."

Important as was Nancy Hanks in the life of her son—his eloquence can be inferred from her brief words of farewell—I have always thought that it was his stepmother, Sarah Bush Lincoln, who encouraged his humor and love of literature. Marrying Thomas, she rescued the Lincolns from their gloom, pulled the family together, and gave Abraham the confidence he needed to embrace the world. Otherwise, he might have made his life around cabins similar to these.

Not finding nearby either a campground or a motel for the night, I drove toward Bardstown, passing the Lincoln Homestead State Park Golf Course, further proof that he was an important founder of the Republican party. I knew Bardstown from a radio interview I had done about the Bourbon industry. Many distillers are located in or around the town, and apparently they dole out shots to tourists. I have never had much of a taste for Bourbon, although that may be for the same reason that Robert E. Lee was ambivalent about war ("that . . . we should grow too fond of it"). I liked the sound of Bardstown from its Internet profiles and decided to stay there for the night, or at least stop for dinner.

Just before dark, I found a campground in the center of Bardstown and pulled up to the office to pay for a night. An attendant was on duty in a small hut. When I asked him about the weather that evening, he spoke of possible tornadoes in the area and encouraged me to stay indoors. I thanked him for the warning, but then wasn't sure whether I should find a hotel in town or push on to Lexington.

With taverns, pubs, ye-olde-hotels, and formal gardens around the Bourbon businesses, Bardstown struck me as the kind of place you came with your spouse or partner on a weekend. I didn't think the hotels would have what my father used to call "a commercial single." I made some loops around town in the car, and when the skies opened up I decided to find a hotel in Lexington and got on the interstate for the 60-mile drive to the city where Lincoln's future wife, Mary Todd, grew up.

In the rain and darkness, with no clue about the layout of Lexington, I drove directly into the downtown, only to ricochet to an interstate exchange where all the motels are located. It was well past 10 p.m. when I finally checked in, and too late for dinner. The motel had nothing to eat, and I could not face driving in the rain to an Outback Steakhouse. I ate apples from my cooler and set my sights on a full breakfast in the morning and a visit to the house of Henry Clay, known as Ashland.

Henry Clay's Ashland:
In search of Lincoln's hero

THE MANAGER AT THE CAMPGROUND had predicted the weather, as at daybreak rain was coming down sideways. I got soaked running from the room to the car and then into the Waffle House. I was well beyond the districts that might have a country kitchen or warm biscuits, and I ate sullenly while figuring out on the map how to get to Ashland. Because it did not open until 10 a.m., I drove around the University of Kentucky and ran through the raindrops to the bookstore, which struck me as long on Kentucky sweatshirts and short on books that should be read in college. I had a coffee on campus and then turned up at Ashland, where I was told that because of the weather the first tour would start only at 11 a.m. I was welcome to watch the film about Clay's life and, as the rain had let up, stroll in the gardens.

The video presented Clay as a Great American who had served his country in the House and Senate, nearly been elected president on several occasions, and, in moments of personal crisis, retreated to the happy confines of Ashland, to compose historic legislation (the Missouri Compromise) or pace reflectively around the planation.

Out in the garden, I chatted with some of the volunteers from the Lexington Garden Club, who were pulling weeds from the great man's rose garden. They appeared to be socially prominent women with green thumbs. One of them, Cathy Brooks, said she was distantly related to Mary Todd and that I should not miss the family house in downtown Lexington.

By the time the Ashland tour started, I had lost my earlier interest in Clay. I was annoyed at all the rules that governed visits to his house, and to some extent I still had a quarrel with his hawking for the War of 1812. Later I tried to read several Clay biographies, figuring I would warm to his life story after the visit to Ashland. Such an approach had worked with the life of Patrick Henry, after I went around Red Hill. Then it turned out that Clay's son James Brown Clay had torn down the original Ashland—the house that had welcomed James Monroe, Daniel Webster, and the Marquis de Lafayette—and replaced it with this Italianate "pile," which looks like a fraternity house.

Clay might have been the only American who, as president, could have avoided the Civil War, and I appreciated him as Lincoln's political hero. I did not, however, buy into the Ashland story or any of the expensive books on sale in the gift shop. When I could break away from the explanations about the china or the Compromise of 1850 (both struck me as cracked), I drove downtown and parked behind the Mary Todd Lincoln House, where Clay again became a political inspiration, not a caricature on a house tour.

Mary Todd Lincoln:
"She tried too hard"

MARY TODD LINCOLN IS REMEMBERED in American history for going mad in the White House. She grew up in Lexington, in this brick house on West Main Street, although she met Lincoln while she was living with her sister in Springfield, Illinois, and he was an emerging lawyer and political figure. Clearly, Lincoln understood the advantages of marrying into a socially prominent family in Lexington. Did they wonder, at least initially, why she had fallen in love with a railsplitter from Hodgenville?

Although top billing for the Lexington house is now given to Mary Todd Lincoln, the more rightful proprietor was her stepmother, Elizabeth Humphreys, who loved Mary's father more than his children. In her house they were treated as boarders more than family. It is little wonder that Mary Todd moved in with her sister in Springfield, and that after her marriage in 1842, she and Abe spent little time at the house in Lexington. The notable exception was a three-week stay in 1847, after Lincoln had been elected to Congress, and the young couple stopped to visit her father. It was on that visit that Henry Clay gave a speech in Lexington, at which

Lincoln may or may not have been in attendance (I believe he was). If so, it would have been the only time he saw his political mentor in person.

The Todd house tour focused more on the china and the wallpaper than on the politics of the Whig party. Afterward I walked with the guide back to the bookshop and asked her to recommend a Mary Todd Lincoln biography. She suggested *The Lincolns: Portrait of a Marriage* by Daniel Mark Epstein, which I bought in the gift shop and read with interest when back home in Europe. Until the visit, I had known little about Lincoln's wife, other than the usual rumors about her madness and bizarre personality. Lincoln's secretaries, John G. Nicolay and John Hay, called her "the hellcat" or "Her Satanic Majesty."

After reading the biography, I found myself sympathetic about the Lincolns' marriage and more understanding of what today we might call Mary Todd's bipolar nature. Because of Mary Todd, I also softened my views about Henry Clay, the political hero of her family and husband. At his 1847 speech in Lexington, Clay broke with the administration's war policies in Mexico, even though his son had died in the fighting. Epstein writes:

> His own son, Henry Clay, Jr., had died valiantly on a Mexican battlefield, and yet the old man was willing to call the motives of his country into question. 'How did we unhappily get involved in this war? It was predicted as the consequence of the annexation of Texas to the United States. If we had not Texas, we should have no war.'

Later Clay said, in words that would have inspired the antiwar Mary: "Of all the dangers and misfortunes which could befall this nation, I should regard that of its becoming a warlike and conquering power the most direful and fatal."

My guess is that the young Mary Todd, the woman Lincoln fell in love with and married, was sprightly and sharp, witty and opinionated. I can see her holding her own with Lincoln in political conversation, even challenging the lesser angels of his nature. There's a bit of Sarah Bush Lincoln in Mary, wanting the Lincolns to be surrounded by nice furniture and a stately home. (Left on his own, I suspect Lincoln's room would have looked like *The Odd Couple*'s Oscar Madison's, although with more copies of Shakespeare than *Sports Illustrated*.)

Mary would have been a political wife, up on the gossip in Springfield or Washington. She would have pushed her husband to seek higher office, confident in his abilities to persuade and lead. The effects of four childbirths, however, and the loss of her son Eddie to tuberculosis in 1850 shifted the trains of her mind onto any number of dark sidetracks.

Epstein writes that she had "an emotional temperament much like an April day, laughing one moment and crying the next" and that after Tad's birth in 1853 she "began to lose control over her actions." The closer Abraham Lincoln drew to national politics, the more she resented having to share him with the larger world. "Politics," Epstein noted, "which had always drawn the Lincolns together, now became a source of discord."

As First Lady, Mary Todd Lincoln, to use an expression I heard from the gardeners at Ashland, "tried too hard" to be accepted in Washington's social establishment, and it rejected her. In response, she went on wild shopping sprees, ostensibly to make over the dreary White House (James Buchanan had been a bachelor there and Lincoln himself called it a "third-rate hotel"), but the results only contributed to the world of Washington gossip. Epstein writes: "She was establishing a reputation as a loose cannon, first for the frankness of her political opinions, and now for her freedom of movement in public, where every gesture of the president-elect's wife was subject to hard scrutiny." She traveled to New York without her husband; she took vacations by herself in Long Branch, New Jersey.

The Civil War, involving her family on the Confederate side, and then the death of her beloved Willie at age twelve pushed her over an emotional edge. Epstein recounts:

> In 1861 Lincoln had risen to a position where his strengths of character came to the fore and flourished, while his wife, deprived of his attention and guidance, succumbed to her weaknesses. Acquisitive, she now had unlimited means to acquire; vulnerable to flattery, she was now set upon by a host of professional sycophants, affable serpents; hungry for social influence, she now occupied a high seat of power where the social fabric intertwined with the political.

Two years later, according to Epstein, she began "to experience the delusions and hallucinations of what now would be diagnosed as clinical psychosis, and the signs were heartbreaking for those who loved her." Her husband tried to jolly her along and protect her from the encroaching world and madness, but he was prosecuting a war that had taken three of her brothers and a brother-in-law. When Grant turned south at the Wilderness and Spotsylvania, after losing so many men, she said in disgust: "He is a butcher, and is not fit to be at the head of an army." At the same time, her husband was saying, "I can't spare this man. He fights." Dinners in the White House cannot have been easy, although I believe Lincoln loved her until his end.

Keeneland, Kentucky:
Midway's soda shop

BEFORE LEAVING LEXINGTON, I wanted to get a look at the bluegrass horse barns and peek into the track at Keeneland, which my friend Charlie Harris had often described to me. He was sick with cancer in New York City, and together we were working on his book *Incurable*, about his life after diagnosis with the disease. He had often written about the track and the surrounding barns. By touring around them I hoped I would be sending Charlie a message of friendship, even though tracks and horse racing have never held much interest for me. I found Keeneland on a local map (naturally, on Man o' War Boulevard) and picked up a road sign for it, just past the Mary Todd Lincoln House.

Parking was easy, although in a paddock of mud from all the rain, and I paid $5 for an entrance ticket. The goal is to make money on bad bets, not up front on ticket prices. I decided to forgo a program, as my decision was to stay for only one race, bet on number three, watch the horses run, and leave, which is what I did. Even if number three finished last, I did enjoy watching the trainers walk their horses outside the track. Up close, a thoroughbred reminds me of bronze sculpture, perhaps one by Edgar Degas, who in his work made the connection between ballet dancers ready to leap and horses set to run.

I had thought that the barn country around Keeneland might be a place to ride my bike, except that the torrential rains were back. I settled for a drive around bluegrass country. As I was on the lookout for Calumet Farms (the only thoroughbred barn I have heard of), a phone call came through from my lawyers, asking me if I could respond to a document they had sent me that morning. I had left the motel before it arrived, and now in the car had no way to connect to the Internet. I said I would scout around for a hot spot and send through my corrections. Anyone who has ever been involved in a lawsuit knows that most of the time is spent proofreading documents, and my case was no exception.

I did not mind answering the request, as I admire the lawyers on my case. I had a moment of panic about finding wi-fi in the middle of horse country, where there are many graceful paddocks but no Starbucks. I drove toward the interstate, figuring something along it would be wired. Instead I stumbled into the delightful village of Midway, where a single line of track bisects the main street, and on either side of the railroad there are cafés, bookstores, and antique shops. Never was a tourist town more welcome. I settled into a retro soda shop, not just for its wi-fi, but for lunch, coffee, dessert, and a newspaper.

Wayne, West Virginia:
"Taylor's been expecting you"

I WAS SPENDING THE NIGHT IN WAYNE, West Virginia, with Taylor Maynard, the grandfather of my daughter's college roommate. I was due sometime after 5 p.m. By taking the interstate instead of the old country road through Morehead, I figured I would be there on time. On a school holiday with her roommate, my daughter had stayed with "Grampa Taylor" and loved his company, and, even though we had never met, Taylor's daughter Suzanne encouraged me to stay with her father.

Wayne is south of Interstate 64, near Huntington, West Virginia, where I took pictures of the Ohio River and toured around Marshall University (football stars Chad Pennington and Randy Moss were the only graduates I had heard of). Wayne is not well marked on Highway 152, but after about fifteen miles I drove into the small West Virginia town and began the hunt for Taylor's house. It was another case where GPS might have saved me from wrong turns but also the sometime pleasures of getting lost. In this case, my directions called for a turn after a motel, but when I could not find it I went back to the motel, to ask some people out front if they knew the street. Right away, the woman I asked said: "Are you Matthew? Taylor's been expecting you."

I liked Taylor immediately. He lives alone in a spacious house in a new development, but his relatives keep an eye out for him. One of them was there when I arrived, and he slipped some frozen dinners into the microwave. The three of us ate at the kitchen table, and then settled into the living room, where the television was on in the background but the conversation took center stage.

A man in his late eighties, Taylor is ebullient, witty, smart, direct, and engaging. He grew up in West Virginia, not far from Wayne, but spent his adult life elsewhere before coming home. Sometimes, he would make comments to the television, as when Donald Trump appeared on screen and Taylor adopted the voice of Trump to say playfully, "You're fired!"

We spent time talking about business and stocks, as Taylor had the television set to a cable business network, and people were on the air to talk about the gold market or bear traps. I got the impression that Taylor managed his money almost as a day trader, and must have been doing well, as he was alert to all the buy and sell signals, and knew the quotes on stocks like Johnson & Johnson as precisely as his blood pressure. "Well," he said, "I'd trade that index [his blood pressure], but no one will let me."

Outside the house, he got around the garden on a motorized scooter, and the next morning, over coffee, he talked about World War II. I can't remember who first raised the topic, but at this point our conversations were far-ranging, and I think I must have followed up something he said about the war.

Taylor had been a private in the Army's First Division—as he said, "the Big Red One." I don't recall that he had landed on D-Day, but he was fighting close to the Rhine one day when his sergeant ordered him and several other men to take out a German machine gun nest. "Well," he said, "I took off and got around behind them, but when I looked back, I could see that none of the others had come with me. So I took care of the machine gun, and then somehow got back to our lines." For that action, Taylor was awarded the Silver Star for valor in combat. He also won a Bronze Star, but I never heard the details of that commendation. After the war, he settled into civilian life and raised his family. I wondered how many of his friends and family knew that he had been among the most decorated soldiers in the European war.

Taylor's brother had died that week, and relatives were coming by that morning to take him to the funeral. We said goodbye in the driveway, with me promising to return, and I was immediately confronted with my route choice for the day. In a general sense, I was heading back to the Northeast, and my life of the lawsuit and parental cares. But I still had a little more time on the road, and I wanted to take the interstate from Charleston to Morgantown and east to Hagerstown.

I had not been in West Virginia since spring 1972, and I was determined to make the most of the day. I decided to cut across the state to see the sites of the principal Civil War battles that were fought in West Virginia. The problem was that my long conversations with Taylor had kept me from my maps, and I had yet to connect the dots between Gauley Bridge, Carnifex Ferry, and Droop Mountain—sites of three important battles. Leaving Wayne, I felt like I was a taking a shot in the dark.

The Civil War Comes to West Virginia:
A gorge of Yangtze proportions

Driving to Charleston to see the state capitol, I brooded on the problem until I stopped for gas and made the quick decision to drive on Highway 60, which runs along the Kanawha River. Traveling without a guidebook, at least one that discussed options beyond the Civil War, I looked up the river in Keegan's Civil War history, which I had on the front seat, and found this:

> The Great Kanawha river is one of the few which crosses the Appalachian chain; it rises in North Carolina and feeds the Ohio River. On it stands Charleston, capital of what is today West Virginia, and, eventually Pittsburgh, at the spot where it is joined by the Monongahela. Physically the Great Kanawha is a major waterway, but in the nineteenth century the terrain it flowed through was undeveloped, with few towns or road and no railroads.

Such an endorsement was too good to ignore, and after some loops around Charleston, and with a full tank of gas, I headed south by southeast, first through the industrial suburbs of the capital (and Randy Moss's hometown), and then along a two-lane road that hugged a riverbank as pretty as any on my trip. Why had I never heard anyone sing the praises of the Kanawha for its reach and beauty? I stopped for pictures of the Glen Ferris Inn, should someday I cajole my wife to join me on a tour of the river (although I may have to play down the importance of Randy Moss when talking up the excursion).

At the Battle of Gauley Bridge, Confederate and Union forces tangled for control of the junction where the Gauley and New Gauley rivers flow into the Kanawha. In 1861, desperate for any kind of success, Lincoln and his commanders sought to liberate the western Virginia counties from the Confederacy, and they dispatched troops from the western theater to push into the valleys. For a while, the West Virginia theater featured several generals who were destined for bigger commands, although the fighting here masked their true abilities.

In summer 1861, General George McClellan won the first battle in western Virginia, at the classical-sounding Philippi, which is near Clarksburg, in the northern part of the state. That victory put him on the radar for senior command, although in time Lincoln would despair of his many hesitations and relieve him after Antietam. (The president wrote: "I have just read your despatch about sore-tongued and fatigued horses. Will you pardon me for asking what the horses of your army have done since the battle of Antietam that fatigues anything?")

Equally misleading in West Virginia was the lackluster performance of Robert E. Lee in the 1861 battle of Cheat Mountain. That defeat prompted President Jefferson Davis to transfer Lee to a near-useless command of the coastline in the Carolinas. Less than a year later, both generals would be in command of their respective armies and facing each other for months in northern Virginia, where Lee shone and McClellan remained "horse-tired." Before Lee won fame, a contemporary had said of him: "He will take more chances, and take them quicker, than any other general in the country—North or South."

I pulled the car over at Gauley Bridge, and saw where the Union forces had scattered the Confederates, taking the bridge and securing their hold on the Kanawha Valley. While more than 5,000 troops were involved on both sides, the battle was more a skirmish. The main event took place a week later at Carnifex Ferry, where I headed next, thinking it was a short drive from the bridge. While the Confederates had marched along the Gauley River to an encampment at Carnifex Ferry, I had to make a long detour of some twenty miles on Highway 19 to get to the state park. It was one of those drives that looks close on a map, but still takes an hour. At least I drove through Hawks Nest State Park, a dramatic gorge of Yangtze proportions along the Kanawha, and Ansted, where Stonewall Jackson's mother is buried.

When I pulled into the Carnifex battlefield park, I realized that I should have stopped for lunch before heading toward the battlefield, which is above the river and a mile from the ferry crossing. The park was out of season and desolate, and cold winds were whipping through the trees on the bluff that looks down to the ferry, where most of the fighting took place. I improvised lunch from my cooler—more peanut butter and apples, as I could never figure out shopping on this trip—and took pictures of a house that was at the center of the one-day battle.

Union General William Rosecrans led his 7,000 men from Clarksburg down to Carnifex Ferry and surprised the Confederates, led by General John Floyd, who were in bivouac around what is called the Patterson House, a simple frame dwelling that stands as a memorial to the fighting. Rosecrans' men outnumbered those of Floyd, and suffered more casualties in the fighting, but the battle was decisive in securing independence for the western counties of Virginia. In many respects West Virginia's statehood can be traced to the fighting here in September 1861, although I would have thought more of its significance had it been open for lunch and the air warmer.

Rosecrans had a long Civil War career in the western campaigns, and even replaced General Don Carlos Buell after the latter was dismissed for his incompetence (or deafness) at Perryville. Rosecrans himself was cashiered after the disastrous battles around Chattanooga, notably Chickamauga. Grant relieved him of his command and later wrote in his memoirs: "Although he showed some strategic ability in his advance, Rosecrans proved a poor tactical leader in the field." His performance at Carnifex Ferry gave some hints of that, but so few were Union victories in the early years of the war that in 1863 Lincoln sent a confidant, James R. Gilmore, to sound out "Old Rosey" about running with him as the vice presidential nominee in the 1864 election. Nothing came of the feeler, and Lincoln ran with Andrew Johnson of Tennessee against another general who frustrated the president in battle, George McClellan.

General Robert E. Lee:
"His sightliness, politeness, and unimpeachability"

FROM THE PARK, I HEADED EAST across the Monongahela National Forest, which had proved almost the undoing of Robert E. Lee's career at Cheat Mountain. I had thought of turning north on Route 150 and seeing if I could find what remains on that mountain, but at the time I knew even less about Lee's campaign there than at Droop Mountain, where I was headed.

Driving east, and with nothing on the car radio in such a digital void, I thought about Lee, wondering if he was as great a general as history has decided. He did, much more than Lincoln, have an ability to surround himself with capable generals. Jackson and Longstreet, for example, were greater than McClellan and Meade (the latter of whom was, according to one subordinate, "that damned old goggle eyed snapping turtle"). Only the combination late in the war of Grant and Sherman, plus the weight of Northern industrial production, bested the chivalric duo of Lee and Jackson. Lee was the master tactician, at his best once the first guns had sounded. He understood his opponents, divided his forces, if need be, instinctively (as happened at Chancellorsville), and he could move divisions around as easily as chess pieces. As a strategist, however, he wasn't much better than his record in West Virginia showed.

My problem with Lee's greatness is that I cannot fathom the cause for which he led so many men to their deaths. Yes, he believed in Virginia more than in the federal government of the United States, and he saw a form of liberty or regional democracy in the Confederacy. But hanging onto slavery wasn't much of a war aim, and I sense that once the fighting began, Lee was in the thick of it because it was the greatest game of all.

His vision of the Civil War stretched little beyond the fields of battle—the hills around Fredericksburg or the mule shoe at Spotsylvania—like some football coach concerned only with winning on Sunday. His invasions of Maryland in 1862 and Pennsylvania in 1863 were doomed, if not to failure, then to the exhaustion of his armies. Would burning the railroad bridges at Harrisburg really have cut the Union in two? He was styled as a defensive genius, but then bet the plantations on stretching his lines from Vicksburg to Gettysburg and lost to a general, Grant, whose strategic imagination was limited to stubbornness. (After a disastrous first day at Shiloh, Grant said to Sherman: "Yes. Lick 'em tomorrow, though.")

In his elegant short biography of General Lee, Roy Blount Jr. concludes: "The consensus in recent years seems to have swung toward Grant's postbellum assessment (in which one of Lee's top lieutenants, James Longstreet, concurred): Lee was a great defensive general but on offense he got away with murder, so to speak, until he didn't any more." Blount quotes Lee's nephew, whom he calls "the otherwise reverent Fitzhugh Lee":

Lee's only weakness as a commander . . . was his "reluctance to oppose the wishes of others, or to order them to do anything that would be disagreeable and to which they would not consent." With men as well as with women, his authority derived from his sightliness, politeness, and unimpeachability.

Those qualities may explain why he had better chemistry with the passionate Jackson as opposed to the dyspeptic Longstreet. They needed few words to understand each other. Jackson could put into action the little that Lee said. Lee came apart on the third day of Gettysburg, when Longstreet was counseling a strategic withdrawal. Instead, Lee sent General George Pickett into the center of the Union lines. Blount writes: "As an attacking general he was inspiring but not necessarily cogent." He also asks: "Why did Lee stake everything, finally, on an ill-considered thrust straight up the middle?"

The Greenbrier Valley:
"Born into a family of ghosts"

ACROSS THE WOODS and into the Greenbrier Valley I found the temperatures moderating and the winds decreasing. Finally it felt like springtime in Virginia, although technically I was still in West Virginia. I turned right off the park road and in a few miles found the birthplace of the writer Pearl Buck, who was born in Hillsboro before her family moved to China, where she achieved her fame as an author. She won the Nobel Prize for Literature for *The Good Earth* and other sympathetic accounts of rural China. Her birthplace is a large white house, both simple and adorned with columns, that sits back from the road on farmland that merges with the broader Greenbrier Valley. Hoping to get inside, I rang the bell and knocked on the doors, in disbelief that it would be closed on a weekday afternoon in springtime.

Thinking maybe the curator was away for lunch, I drove down the road to the Hillsboro Public Library and asked at the desk if the writer's home was open. The librarian said that normally it was, but that the volunteer was sick that day. Instead he showed me a book, *Pearl Buck in China: Journey to the Good Earth* by Hilary Spurling, which begins: "Pearl

Sydenstricker [her birth name] was born into a family of ghosts," although mostly they were American missionaries, originally from Hillsboro. I sense that her books, once so popular, have lost their audience, evoking a Christian benevolence toward the rural Chinese—Ayn Rand meets Chinese warlordism—while the new China is more a socialist chop shop of modern capitalism.

Down the road from the library, I spotted the Hillsboro Café, in the procession of local restaurants on this trip that began in Appomattox at Baine's and continued into Rural Retreat, Cumberland, and Midway. This café was combined with a small grocery, bakery, and antiques store, plus books and other local items for sale. (I bought a handmade straw pot scrubber that came on a wrought-iron hook, and some rustic nails.) Hungry from my early start in Wayne, I ordered a hamburger and salad, and lingered at the table with my computer and coffee. Only reluctantly did I leave in mid-afternoon, as I wanted to see the Civil War battlefield of Droop Mountain and the famous Greenbrier resort.

Droop Mountain State Park has one of those observation towers where it is possible to climb a set of wooden stairs and survey the sweep of the battlefield. The "mountain" is more a large hill, but it cuts across the Greenbrier Valley south of Hillsboro. In November 1863, a Union brigade was headed south with the idea of disrupting the rail lines between Virginia and Tennessee, and it ran into entrenched Confederate forces on Droop Mountain's high ground.

From the watchtower, it seemed to me impossible that Union forces could have turned the Confederate lines, as they had to ascend a hill more stout than Marye's Heights and fight in thick woods like those at the Wilderness. That, however, is exactly what happened, and the broken Confederates retreated down the valley to Virginia, never again threatening the Union presence in West Virginia.

I followed the Confederate line of retreat, although mine ended at The Greenbrier resort in White Sulphur Springs, once the crown jewel resort of the Chesapeake & Ohio Railway, when holidays involved trains and suites were staffed with butlers. I was more interested in the railway part of the hotel, and found the station in a parking lot across the street. I read my book in the sun and walked around the gardens. Inside, the feel is that of a corporate convention center, as the door attendants were hefting large golf bags out of late-model sedans and pushing carts piled high with Vuitton luggage.

I had wondered briefly if maybe I should stay at the Greenbrier. Perhaps the Internet might have some off-season bargain rate? That notion, however, passed when I saw that a simple room was $335 a night, before tax, tips, dinner, and breakfast. Nor did I find myself warming to the Greenbrier, which is the size of a Russian sanatorium. I preferred my new Walmart cot and sleeping bag to a corporate suite.

Instead of checking in, I decided to push over the Appalachians to Lexington, Virginia, where I could wallow in the departed spirits of Robert E. Lee and Stonewall Jackson. Before the war, Jackson was an instructor at the Virginia Military Institute (VMI) in Lexington, and after the war Lee was the president of Washington College, renamed Washington and Lee after he died.

The drive was sixty miles to Lexington, and the interstate through the mountains was free of traffic and offered stunning views. Because it was early evening, I decided to park near the two colleges, which are side by side, and bike around the town at dusk. I could find the house where Jackson had lived with his wife, see VMI, and maybe get into the chapel where Lee's remains are buried, as close as American history gets to a Napoleonic tomb. According to legend, his last words were "Strike the tent!"

For once on the trip, I was riding without the threat of rain, and at sunset, Lexington's red bricks glowed in the fading light. Track and field was being practiced at the stadium, and the sound of baseball mixed with the canned music that has become the necessary compliment to exercise. Jackson's house is in the downtown section, a row house that boasts a gift shop, parking, and a museum. They were closed, but I took pictures and read plaques telling about the man and the myth, both of which can be consumed during business hours.

Lexington, Virginia:
Stonewall Jackson's questions of confidence

How did Thomas Jackson, a not very dynamic lecturer at VMI, turn into the most innovative officer of the Civil War? In the words of historian Shelby Foote in the Ken Burns Civil War documentary, "He was no professor," but inspirational to his cadets, largely because of his "hard-shell" Calvinism. According to Foote, Jackson saw war as "a question of confidence."[8]

Of his single-minded intensity, Mary Chestnut writes in her diary (as quoted in Blount): "Jackson was a one-idea man." His mystical faith, the burning look of righteousness in his eyes, and his endless impatience with cant and roadblocks made him the perfect instrument to carry out Lee's directions—although in many cases I suspect the daring plans came from Jackson, with Lee smiling his affirmation.

On his own, Jackson bedeviled Union forces in the Shenandoah Valley. Lee just sent him there. Jackson liked to say: "Always mystify, mislead, and surprise the enemy, if possible; and when you strike and overcome him, never let up

---

8: In the film, Foote speaks about Chancellorsville in his elegant Southern accent, repeating Jackson's words: "The Institute will be heard from today."

in the pursuit so long as your men have strength to follow; for an army routed, if hotly pursued, becomes panic-stricken, and can then be destroyed by half their number." He also could sound like Mao or Ho Chi Minh, in his embrace of guerrilla tactics:

> The other rule is, never fight against heavy odds, if by any possible maneuvering you can hurl your own force on only a part, and that the weakest part, of your enemy and crush it. Such tactics will win every time, and a small army may thus destroy a large one in detail, and repeated victory will make it invincible.

For the South, at least mythologically, Jackson's death at Chancellorsville set in motion the events that led to defeat at Gettysburg. Had he, not Longstreet, plotted with Lee in the dirt near the Chambersburg Pike, the Union left wing might have been turned on the second day. On the third day he would have devised a plan to hit Meade at "the weakest part," not directly into Cemetery Ridge. Later Lee reflected: "If I had Stonewall Jackson with me, as far as a man can see, I should have won the Battle of Gettysburg." Nor would Lee have bickered with Jackson once the plan was agreed. Jackson, like Lee, came from an earlier age, when war was a blood sport. "As the inelegant Grant and Sherman would prove in the long run," writes Blount, "this was not personal exploits and dashing camaraderie, but hell."

While I was biking around VMI, I chatted with some cadets who appeared headed toward dinner. When I asked them questions, they added "Sir," to each response, telling me that VMI is a private college, not affiliated with the armed forces. Graduates are not assured a commission, and some cadets see VMI as training for business or other careers, not just the military.

I would have liked to see the Institute's museum, but it was closed, as was the chapel at Washington and Lee that has a small Lee museum, an exhibit showing his office as he left it, and a statue of Lee behind the altar "asleep" on the battlefield—an odd pose for someone so alert in action. Nevertheless, I enjoyed my bike ride through Lexington at dusk, although I returned to my parked car with no clear idea where I might stay the night.

Certainly Lexington has many hotels, but I didn't find any as I drove slowly away from the downtown. I kept thinking of the GPS command to "find accommodation." Nor did I pick the right exit off the interstate to find the collection of Interstate motels. In the end I decided to sleep that night up the I-81 line in Staunton, Virginia, to be ready the next morning when the Woodrow Wilson Presidential Library and Birthplace Home opened its doors at 9 a.m. Searching in the darkness for a Days Inn, I remembered what one Union soldier said about Jackson: "Boys, he's not much for looks, but if we'd had him we wouldn't be caught in this mess."

Woodrow Wilson of Staunton, Virginia:
Always a ladies' man

THE FIRST TOUR OF WILSON'S BIRTHPLACE HOME, next to the library, wasn't until 10:00 a.m. so I wandered through the museum to get a sense of how his circle of donors wanted him remembered.

Thomas Woodrow Wilson was born in Staunton in 1856, although a year later his Presbyterian-minister father moved the family to Augusta, Georgia. Late in life, he would recall Sherman's March to the Sea. Augusta is more his home town than Staunton, which Wilson did not remember from his childhood.

During the Civil War, Wilson's father was a chaplain for the Confederate Army, a fact often overlooked in associating Wilson with progressive causes. The son never lost entirely the dismissive racial attitudes he acquired coming of age in the Deep South. From the house tour, what was most apparent is that Wilson's childhood family dinners lasted for hours, while his father lectured about the Bible and led the children in hymns.

Although he was dyslexic, Wilson earned a doctorate in political science and wrote seventeen books, some on an early portable typewriter that he took with him everywhere and pounded at night, after the family had gone to sleep. Woodrow was his mother's maiden name. He adopted it when he began to have political ambitions, beyond those of an academic on the make. When he was a professor at Princeton, for example, he moved a short distance to a house opposite that of the university's president, no doubt to wave cheerfully at his new neighbor. His first wife, Ellen, was from Rome, Georgia, and they had three daughters, two of whom were married in the White House before Ellen died in 1914 of Bright's disease.

Despite the image Wilson cultivated as an austere preacher's son, he was always a ladies' man. On vacation in Bermuda in 1907, he began a passionate affair with Mary Peck that would last many years, until she was divorced from her husband in 1912. Wilson was named in the divorce suit as a co-respondent. During the presidential campaign that year, Wilson's advisors had to pay Mrs. Peck $7,500 to purchase some of the candidate's steamiest letters, which perhaps were also hammered out on his portable typewriter.

Mrs. Peck was further wounded when the widower Wilson chose to marry the younger, flamboyant Edith Bolling Galt in December 1915, after a whirlwind courtship that spawned a popular joke in Washington. Question: "What did Edith Galt do when Wilson proposed to her?" Answer: "She fell out of bed." At the Paris Peace Conference in 1919, there was some speculation that Queen Marie of Romania had worked some of her bedroom charms on Wilson, which may explain why Romania did little for the Allies but ended up acquiring Transylvania and Bessarabia.

Although the museum has copies of Wilson's Fourteen Points (point ten, perhaps for Queen Marie? "Autonomous development for ethnic peoples of Austria-Hungary"), notes that the campaign song in 1912 was "Sit Down and Rock It Out With Me," and reveals that Wilson signed his love letters to Edith as "Tiger," what drew my attention was the saga of his Pierce-Arrow car, now a shiny, white-walled centerpiece of the museum. As president, he used it as his limousine, and on his leaving office, five wealthy Princeton alumni bought the car and made it a gift to Wilson, although not before they removed the U.S. eagle hood ornament, replaced it with a Princeton "Tiger," and painted the trimmings on the car the university colors of orange and black.

In the last years of his life, one of Wilson's few pleasures was motoring around Washington in the Pierce-Arrow, which on his death in 1924 his wife gave to residents in Staunton, who were already eager to organize a museum in their favorite son's honor. Notes on the car indicate: "George Howard (Wilson's chauffeur) drove the car to Staunton and left it with the Reverend A.M. Frasier, the Presbyterian minister, who parked the car in Frasier's neighbor's garage. Stayed there for ten years, while the Wilson National Memorial is created."

The birthplace home did not open until 1941. Meanwhile the Pierce-Arrow was stored in a local Buick dealership. When the car company needed the space, it moved the limo over to the Staunton coliseum, although there it was parked in a dingy storage area and sometimes even out in the fields, where vandals stripped the car's lanterns and (Princeton) hood ornaments. In 1963 the car was sent to New York for an extensive renovation, although the shady garage there again parked it outside and did none of the quoted work. (What did they expect from a New York City body shop?)

Nor could the Pierce-Arrow company help with the restoration, because it had gone out of business in 1938, and its assets were sold in 1940 to Studebaker.

In 1972 the car was sent to Charlottesville, Virginia, to begin the restoration that continued, on and off, for the next twenty years, either to the body or the engine. (In 1973, at a dedication ceremony, the residents of Staunton had to push the car to the museum after the motor gave out.) One of the hood ornaments was even found in the Washington garage where George Howard had parked the car in 1921, and the side lanterns mysteriously were put up for sale on eBay in 2006, when Wilson's foundation bought them.

Little did Wilson know, when he came back to Washington from the Paris Peace Conference to be greeted by the delirium of 100,000 fans at Union Station and a shiny new Pierce-Arrow, that his car would outlast the League of Nations by more than fifty years.

I ended my visits to the museum and the boyhood home in the gift shop, where a number of Wilson biographies were on sale, alongside key chains and postcards. I would have bought a book about Versailles and Queen Marie of Romania, but the gift-shop collection takes a more orthodox view of his presidency.

One reason Wilson lost the fight for American membership in the League of Nations was the determined opposition in the Senate of Henry Cabot Lodge. He despised Wilson, although he would have voted for the Treaty of Versailles if language had been inserted that would have allowed the Congress "by joint resolution" to approve military operations undertaken to "preserve the territorial integrity . . . of any country."

Wilson, however, refused to consider any compromise with the language he brought back from Paris. According to one history of the era, *First Great Triumph: How Five Americans Made Their Country a World Power* by Warren Zimmerman, another reason the treaty failed in the Senate was that the austere Lodge could not forgive Wilson for his dalliances, first with Mrs. Peck and later with Edith Galt.

In his own marriage, Lodge had seen his wife, Nannie, conduct a public and passionate affair with Secretary of State John Hay, whom Lodge had recommended to President McKinley for his cabinet in 1897. (A biography of Hay's friend Henry Adams says, "Everyone in Cleveland except Hay's wife knew about it.") Fast-forward to 1914-15, when Lodge's wife died about the same time as Ellen Wilson. Although Nannie Lodge had played the senator for a cuckold (an odd romance covered in Patricia O'Toole's *The Five of Hearts*), Lodge grieved over her loss, apparently much longer than did the widowed president for his departed wife.

While the president was conducting his infatuated courtship of Edith Galt (the head of the Secret Service wrote: "He's hooked hard and fast, and acts like a schoolboy in his first love experience"), Lodge stewed over Wilson's apparent lack of grief. In Wilson's pious pronouncements ("He kept us out of war"), Lodge might have heard some of the same change-the-world formulas that John Hay had uttered while secretary of state and his wife's paramour. For whatever reason, Wilson became a hood ornament for Lodge's anger, and the Versailles treaty became yet another of Wilson's love letters that his lawyers had a hard time explaining.

Harrisburg, Pennsylvania:
Going for broke on the Civil War

FROM STAUNTON, I headed down the Shenandoah Valley, Jackson's "avenue of advance," with my thoughts turning toward my father's home in New Jersey. I wasn't quite ready to end my wanderings, although the weather had turned nasty—at this point a hard, cold rain—and emails from my lawyers and family indicated that my escape time was nearly up.

Looking at the map, I wanted to end the trip in Harrisburg or Gettysburg, although that would be more than a three-hour drive from Staunton. From motel television that morning, I knew that the low standards of the trip's weather would be getting worse, which meant that my hopes of a bike ride around the Gettysburg battlefield might be a stretch. (I felt like Wilson: "riding in his car was one of his few hobbies.") Nor could I do much more on the interstate drive north than spin the radio dial and think about the campaigns that had haunted the Shenandoah. Jackson said: "If this Valley is lost, Virginia is lost." Later Grant said to General Philip Sheridan (veteran of Perryville and—are you surprised?—his widow moved to Saltville): "Do all the damage to railroads and crops you can. Carry off all stock of all descriptions . . . so as to prevent further planting. If the war is to last another year, we want the Shenandoah Valley to remain a barren waste."

Before heading to Gettysburg, I made a side trip to Harrisburg to see my friend Tom Leonard and to go with him to the new Civil War museum. The museum is situated on a bluff in Harrisburg and, according to Tom, it cost about $35 million (which the bankrupt city did not have) to put up the modern building and stuff it full of Civil War artifacts. It was suggested that the former mayor, Steve Reed, had pushed the project because he wanted the pleasure of shopping for muskets with public money—and this in a city with only faint connections to the war. (From Chambersburg, Lee wanted to burn the bridges across the Susquehanna River, but Gettysburg got in the way.)

The museum tells the story of the Civil War, largely at the grade-school level, with timelines and well-lit cabinets that look as though Reed had purchased the entire contents of the collection from some Sotheby's auction, perhaps entitled "Treasures of the Civil War." I saw Lincoln's hat box, George McClellan's saddle, a hat worn by George Pickett; many rifles, swords, and pistols; Stonewall Jackson's glove; a saddle box with Grant's name on the side; Lee's Bible; and a ticket to "Our American Cousin" at Ford's Theater (maybe the one that Grant fobbed off on Major Rathbone?). Had I started here, I might have spent more time with the exhibits. By this point, however, the museum reminded me that for many, collecting Civil War memorabilia is close to an addiction, one that in this case the taxpayers in Harrisburg had enabled.

Besides finally seeing the pen used to sign John Brown's death warrant, I am grateful to the museum for having in its bookshop a copy of *The Impending Crisis: America Before the War 1848-1861* by David M. Potter. I wanted a better explanation of the war's causes, beyond the usual sound-bites about slavery, Lincoln's election, states' rights, and the Nullification Crisis. I was looking for a book that challenged many of the assumptions about the reasons for the conflict. When I read Potter's history, it did not disappoint.

Potter was a professor of history at Yale and Stanford who died in 1971 while working on *The Impending Crisis*. A contemporary, Don Fehrenbacher, completed the project. The book was published in 1976 and was awarded the Pulitzer Prize a year later. The book ends with the words "Slavery was dead; secession was dead; and six hundred thousand men were dead. That was the basic balance sheet of the sectional conflict." What led to the fighting was a political drift that fits few of the stereotypes about the war, especially those on display at the National Civil War Museum.

First up on Potter's list of misunderstood causes of the war is the Wilmot Proviso, a crafty piece of legislation that was attached to an 1846 bill appropriating funds for the Mexican War. It would have banned slavery for any territory seized from Mexico in the fighting that was then two months old. "Since it was a foregone conclusion that the treaty could never command a two-thirds majority in this form," Potter writes, "the introduction of this measure placed Whigs who opposed both annexation and the war in the dilemma that to end the war, they would have to accept annexation, or to prevent annexation they would have to prolong the war." Although it was reintroduced several times, the proviso never passed, although it reintroduced the slavery issue into national politics (dormant since the Missouri Compromise, which the proviso threatened to overturn) and it divided both national parties, Democratic and Whig, into pro- and anti-slavery factions, making later splits inevitable.

To calm the suddenly agitated waters, Henry Clay and others stitched together the Compromise of 1850, intended to paper over the problem of slavery in territories that were being considered for statehood. Potter explains: "The purpose was to put a stop to the agitation of the slavery question. But to accomplish this, the compromisers adopted a law to activate the recapture of fugitive slaves. Here was a firebrand vastly more inflammatory than the Wilmot Proviso."

Unfortunately, the new legislation evaded most of the hard slavery questions, hoping that the courts or territorial legislatures would do what Congress wished to avoid. Potter writes:

> In so far as the territorial question was evaded by leaving it to the courts, the settlement of 1850, for all its apparent concreteness, closely resembled the Clayton Compromise of two years before, which, Thomas Corwin had said, proposed to enact a lawsuit instead of a law.

More important in the 1850s than the question of slavery in the territories was the money of the railroads, which among others had Stephen A. Douglas and Abraham Lincoln in their pockets. The moneyed interests of a transcontinental railroad meant that the questions of slavery in the territories had to be resolved, and one effort to do that was the Kansas-Nebraska Act, which on the moral high road addressed slavery in those territories.

At the retail level of politics (think of suitcases filled with cash), the act was an effort to steer the transcontinental railroad through friendly congressional districts. "In the era of many futile measures," Potter notes, "the Kansas-Nebraska Act approached the apex of futility," and he describes the motivations of Stephen Douglas in terms less lofty than his ruminations in later Lincoln-Douglas debates:

> If he did not himself proclaim his intention to use Kansas-Nebraska as a stepping-stone toward the realization of a railroad by the central or northern route, it was because he would not do so without admitting that he had baited his bill with the meat of repeal of the Missouri Compromise in order to entice the southerners into supporting his schedule to win the Pacific Railroad for his own region.

Douglas skirted the issue of a slavery ban in the territories and stayed true to his Democratic principles, by arguing for "popular sovereignty," which was code that promised to remove the slavery issue as a national question (the states would decide for themselves). Potter describes how Douglas threaded this needle: "Thus, without much concern for the slaves, and without believing that the slavery issue was worth a political crisis, Douglas did regard the restriction of slavery as desirable, and thought of popular sovereignty as an effective device by which to restrict it without precipitating a constant running battle in Congress."

The proxy confrontation, before the Civil War, was over the issue of whether Kansas should be a free or slave state.

Potter is at his best in explaining that the dispute there was fought on false pretenses. He writes:

> The great anomaly of "Bleeding Kansas" is that the slavery issue reached a condition of intolerable tension and violence for the first time in an area where a majority of the inhabitants apparently did not care very much one way or the other about slavery.

Nor does Potter believe that the Dred Scott decision had the import which it carries today in the texts of high school American history classes. He observes:

> Probably no other major judicial decision in history affected the daily lives of as few people as this one. It annulled a law which had in fact been repealed three years previously, and it denied freedom to the slaves in an area where there were no slaves.

At the time, Lincoln's views on slavery were "evolving," to use a modern expression, perhaps because he was a railroad lawyer in his run-up to the 1858 election. Dred Scott raised the specter, in Lincoln's mind, that the Court could extend slavery across the nation, although in his published views he said: "What I would most desire is the separation of the white and black races." Not shown in the National Civil War Museum are all the maps and jottings that Lincoln made about where in the Caribbean or Africa freed slaves might be sent.

In popular fiction, Lincoln won the election of 1860 by opposing secession and agreeing to free the slaves, but in fact he won because the Democrats split their votes between those who were pro-slavery (John C. Breckinridge) and those who would have local referendums sort out the problems (Douglas). According to Potter, Lincoln was a "Hurrah!" candidate who during the campaign was under firm instructions from his packagers not to make a speech or write a letter. (On cue at campaign rallies, his supporters would shout "hurrah.") Otherwise, he was invisible, except in campaign ditties and songs.

The likes of Thurlow Weed, a Republican operator who was called the "wizard of the lobby," commanded "oceans of money." Lincoln, writes Potter, "received only 39 percent of the popular vote, which has led some writers to the mistaken belief that he won because his opposition was divided. But this was not the case; he won because his vote was strategically distributed. It was all located where it would count toward electoral votes, and virtually none was 'wasted in the states which he lost.'" He won more votes in the rural North, and did less well in the cities.

By that point, however, the nation was running on parallel tracks, appropriately, as the election featured two railroad lawyers. Potter concludes: "It is not a very serious exaggeration to say the United States was holding two elections simultaneously on November 6, 1860. . . . Each section conducted its campaign very much as if the other section simply wasn't there." Breckinridge ran against Douglas in the South, and won. Douglas ran against Lincoln in the North, and lost.

Potter blames Lincoln, after his election, for making little effort to reach out to Southern leaders or even to travel to meet them. By the time he was sworn into office four months later, seven states had seceded and formed a new government. Potter writes of the interregnum:

The progress of disunion, far from frightening Republicans into offering concessions, gave them additional reason for standing firm—namely, that any yielding to the secessionists would be a surrender to extortion and a subversion of popular government.

By that point, neither side could hear anything but ultimatums from the other. "Lincoln was prepared," Potter writes, "to accept war rather than acknowledge the dissolution of a Federal Union which in Davis's eye had ceased to exist; Davis, in turn, was ready to make war for the territorial integrity of a Southern Confederacy which in Lincoln's eyes had never begun to exist."

Potter's conclusion is that "the Civil War did far more to produce a southern nationalism which flourished in the cult of the Lost Cause than southern nationalism did to produce the war," but in 1861 the armies were on the march, with a logic of their own.

Chambersburg, Pennsylvania:
James Buchanan says goodbye

BEFORE PARTING, Tom and I toured around Chambersburg, southwest of Harrisburg, in the valley that curves around the mountains toward Gettysburg. James Buchanan was born in nearby Mercersburg, and near the academy of the same name the log cabin of his birth is on display. As president, Buchanan was a Southern politician with a northern address (Lancaster, Pennsylvania), and the mixed metaphor of his politics held the Democratic party together until the 1860 election. Buchanan had no wish to stand for re-election, and Douglas took his place on the ticket, although the two men were polar opposites. Potter describes the differences:

> To Douglas, Buchanan seemed a cold, selfish, conventional-minded party hack, domineering, yet at the same time timid and obsequious to the aristocratic southern leaders, and obsessed with party regularity in its most stultifying form. To Buchanan, Douglas seemed a hard-drinking brawler, a political freebooter, an ambitious upstart, a disturber of the peace, and worst of all, a disloyal Democrat who had allied himself with the Republicans against the Lecompton policy of his party's administration.

Buchanan could not wait to leave the presidency, and said to Lincoln on the latter's inauguration day: "If you are as happy entering the presidency as I am leaving it, then you are a very happy man."

Tom and I said goodbye near the town square in Chambersburg, where Lee, in a meeting with General A.P. Hill, made the fateful decision to follow the contours of the valley and turn his army against Meade at Gettysburg. According to a plaque in the square, the decision was taken on June 26, 1863, around 10 a.m., after which Lee made his headquarters near the town center and sent his men down the road that is now Highway 30, on which I also headed to Gettysburg.

In the vanguard was the cavalry of J.E.B. Stuart, on a par with Jackson among Lee's most able lieutenants. Blount writes: "As much as Jackson, Stuart was the heart and soul of Lee's mythic invincibility." Lee said: "He is my eyes." At Gettysburg Stuart was almost as absent as Jackson, first skirmishing to the north while the battle began, and on the last day, out of position behind Union lines to draw troops away from Cemetery Ridge, which were his orders. Lee criticized Stuart for the lack of intelligence and wrote, defensively: "The march toward Gettysburg was conducted more slowly than it would have been had the movements of the Federal Army been known."

My own arrival in Gettysburg along the Chambersburg Pike didn't go much better than Lee's, although I had less at stake. I pulled off the road into McPherson Ridge, but in the driving rain I could not get my bearings on the rest of the battlefield. I knew where it was, although I got sidetracked around the observation tower that sits on top of the fields of battle of the first day. By the time I had straightened out my lines, so to speak, and found my way to the new visitor center, I had fielded a call from my lawyers and run into a traffic jam. Instead of speaking to me about American tragedy and vision—Chamberlain described a return to the battlefield as a "radiant fellowship [with] the fallen"—Gettysburg was beginning to feel like another day at the office.

Fortunately, I had seen Gettysburg on better days, beginning when I went to college at Lewisburg, 135 miles to the north. Several times I had stood where Lincoln delivered his address, and I had hiked on Little Round Top, where the bayonet charge of Joshua Chamberlain's 20th Maine held the Union left, and the entire line, from Confederate envelopment on the second day. (He described the attack: "Desperate as the chances were, there was nothing for it but to take the offensive. I stepped to the colors. The men turned toward me. One word was enough,—BAYONET!") I had also spent time in the Peach Orchard, the "high water mark" of the Confederate charge on day three. Something about the American experience died and was saved in those bleak patches of trees and boulders.

Gettysburg, Pennsylvania:
"General Lee, I have no division"

ON THIS DAY I NEVER DID GET UNTRACKED, although I drove around the stations of the Confederate and Union crosses and, to show appropriate reverence, occasionally parked near one of the markers. If Gettysburg was hidden behind the fog of tourism and rain, at least I had for my guide Professor James McPherson, author of *Battle Cry of Freedom* and, more recently, *Hallowed Ground: A Walk at Gettysburg.* He wasn't seated next to me in the rental car, as I bought the audio edition of his book, to which I listened as I drove around the battlefield and on my way home to New Jersey.

McPherson was until recently a professor of history at Princeton University, where on several occasions I met with him in his office. He was an editor of a series of books about pivotal moments in American history. I had also heard him speak in Princeton about the battle of Antietam as part of a lecture series at the Nassau Club, of which my father was a member.

McPherson has written a number of bestselling books about the Civil War and appeared often on television. In person I found him unassuming, curious, and engaging. He rode a bicycle to his university office (it was leaning against the wall) and talked about the pleasure he found in leading groups of his students or Princeton alumni to places such as Gettysburg or Shiloh. Before I owned a copy of the book, I knew instinctively that *Hallowed Ground* was his personalized walking tour and lecture about the battle of Gettysburg. In the introduction, he says how difficult it is now to imagine the battlefield ("no fewer than thirty-eight orchards existed on what became the battlefield") and tells his listeners "to imagine a cleared field or parklike woodlot where there are thick woods today, or imagine an orchard or a grove where there are none today. Such a feat of imagination is not always easy."

McPherson also provides some guideposts to the fighting. For example, the two sides suffered in total some 50,000 casualties; Gettysburg now has 1,400 monuments; and the park service has posted a sign that reads, "All persons found using firearms on these grounds will be prosecuted with the utmost rigor of the law."

Throughout *Hallowed Ground*, McPherson dispels a number of myths about Gettysburg, such as: Lee did not march on the town because it had a shoe factory; Henry Wentz never shelled his parents' house in the Peach Orchard; and the Barlow-Gordon incident, in which a Confederate general helps to save a wounded Union general and gets word to his wife in the midst of the battle, is, alas, imagined. ("Nevertheless, the story has persisted to this day, told by some guides and swallowed by tourists because they want to believe that the Civil War was an unfortunate disagreement between good and honorable men, not a cataclysmic Armageddon.")

Between the lines, I heard McPherson's book as an explanation, even an indictment, of what caused Lee's defeat at Gettysburg. He starts with the obvious: if on the first day Lee had urged Jackson, instead of Ewell, to attack the Union center above the town (near the observation tower where I stopped), it would have happened. Ewell entered the fight, but too late in the day to be effective, something impossible to believe would have been the case with Jackson.

On the second day, which Chamberlain rescued for the Union on the left flank, Lee ignored the advice from Longstreet to break off the attacks and shift the army to high ground between Meade and the city of Washington. McPherson writes that Longstreet suggested that "Lee move south (toward Washington) and find some good defensive terrain. This maneuver, said Longstreet, would compel Meade to attack the Confederates, who could stand on the defensive and repeat the victories of Second Manassas and Fredericksburg. But Lee's blood was up. He rejected the advice." According to McPherson, Lee's bullheaded answer was: "The enemy is there, and I am going to attack him there."

By this point in the battle, Lee was suffering from a bad stomach and too little sleep, possibly aspects of heart disease, and all he could think to do was order the men forward. On day three, Lee's only suggestion was a reprise thinking from day two: "The enemy is there. I am going to take them where they are."

McPherson describes Pickett's last charge: "It was an awesome spectacle that the participants on both sides remembered until the end of their lives—which for many came within the next half hour." In sending his men straight ahead into a sausage machine, Lee suffered in one day the same number of casualties (about 7,000) that Grant ran up around Cold Harbor. Nevertheless, history calls Grant a butcher, and Lee a courtly Southerner.

At the core of McPherson's view of the battle is Lee's dismissal of Longstreet's observation "that no fifteen thousand men ever arrayed for battle can take that position." Longstreet also said to a subordinate: "I do not want to make this charge. I do not see how it can succeed. I would not make it now but that General Lee has ordered it and expects it." According to McPherson, Lee said to Pickett after the charge: "General Pickett, place your division in the rear of this hill, and be ready to repel the advance of the enemy should they follow up their advantage." Pickett's answer to Lee was: "General Lee, I have no division."[9]

In retrospect, Lincoln's fate became tied to Gettysburg, although at the time he saw it as either a defeat or a missed opportunity.[10] As McPherson recalls, Lincoln said of Meade: "They will be ready to fight a magnificent battle when there is no enemy there to fight," and he wrote to the Union commander: "My dear general, I do not believe you appreciate the magnitude of the misfortune involved in Lee's escape. He was within your easy grasp, and to have closed upon him would in connection with our other late successes, have ended the war. As it is, the war will be prolonged indefinitely. . . . Your golden opportunity is gone, and I am distressed immeasurably because of it." Nevertheless, five months later, with few

9: After the war, Pickett went to see Lee, and while there he made an aside to Colonel John S. Mosby: "That old man . . . had my division massacred at Gettysburg!" To which Mosby replied: "Well, it made you famous."

10: Immediately after, he said of his famous Address: "I failed, I failed, and that is about all that can be said about it."

changes on the battlefield except the fall of Vicksburg, Lincoln had raised the stakes on the casualties, saying they had fallen so "that government of the people, by the people, for the people, shall not perish from the earth."

Only a string of Gettysburgs—the Wilderness, Spotsylvania, Cold Harbor, Petersburg, Sailor's Creek, Atlanta—delivered on Lincoln's promise of constitutional unity, although he is lucky that posterity has chosen to overlook how many defeats and casualties were suffered on his watch. (I am sure Mary's descent into madness was enough of a reminder to her husband.) I appreciate that McPherson ends his book on a high note—"Gettysburg is important not primarily as the high-water mark of the Confederacy, but as the place where 'this nation, under God, shall have a new birth of freedom.'"—although I worry that the gift shops of freedom are selling a brighter story than the fog war. Shortly after the war, the government "by the people, for the people" had Grant's profiteers in power and Jim Crow laws all over the South. As Henry Adams remarked: "The progress of evolution from President Washington to President Grant was alone evidence to upset Darwin."

Homeward Bound:
Acoustical shadows

FROM GETTYSBURG, I took a slow road to York, where Ewell's corps had been headed until Lee called him back to Gettysburg, and merged onto the Pennsylvania Turnpike for the three-hour drive to Princeton, New Jersey. There was more rain and Friday night traffic. Any thought I had about a quick stop to see James Buchanan's house near Lancaster faded into the mists. The diarist George Templeton Strong wrote: "That Buchanan might be hanged under lynch law almost reconciles me to that code."

I had not tired of history so much as I had run out of time. I had lawyers expecting my presence on Monday morning, and in the meantime I wanted to visit with my mother, whose grip on life was winding down. Sunday was Easter, and a family gathering was planned. I knew, also, that my father was eager to hear my stories of the road, and the moment I arrived in Princeton, he would ask about the Hotel Roanoke, the branch line to Abingdon, the mule shoe at Spotsylvania, those coal hollows around Dante, and how the recession was treating Huntington, West Virginia.

At age ninety-two, my father got just as much pleasure from this trip as I did. I might try to skip over some detail, such as where Burnside had crossed the Rappahannock with those pontoon bridges, but he would bring me back to the place with a question ("What was on Burnside's mind when he tried that?"). After a while I figured out that, for the most part, I had been retracing steps that he had made, beginning after the war on his sugar trips to Appalachia. He had walked along Marye's Heights at Fredericksburg, stayed the night in Whitesburg (if not in a campground), stopped at some of the Lincoln cabins near Bardstown, and knew well the failings of General Hooker at Chancellorsville.

By no coincidence, he gave me for my birthday that weekend *Tried by War* by James McPherson, an appreciation of Lincoln's evolution as a commander, and then launched into an assessment of George McClellan, agreeing with McPherson's words that ". . . McClellan's main defect as a military commander [was] an alarmist tendency to inflate enemy strength and intentions." In turn, that led the conversation into an assessment of other generals with inflated reputations, be they Napoleonic marshals or Marine Corps legends. Even though I had driven the length of the Shenandoah Valley, he knew its topography better than I did and had me reaching for an atlas when he asked, "Tell me again about the battles around Winchester," which changed hands seventy-two times during the Civil War.

During the weekend I cleaned out the rental car and put away the mounds of camping gear, little of which I had used. I had not pitched my tent at Perryville or in the Blue Ridge Mountains, and I regretted that the tornadoes and rain had chased me indoors to all those interstate motels. I had biked some, notably at Fredericksburg and Lexington, but I had missed the long ride around the vortex of the Civil War—Chancellorsville, the Wilderness, Spotsylvania, and, of course, Gettysburg. I felt lucky to have gotten my introduction to Anne Caudill and to have seen so much of Harlan County. I was disappointed that Gettysburg had been obscured behind a cavalcade of RVs and cold April rains. I still had not made it to the Civil War theater in the West, places such as Shiloh and Chattanooga, but at least at Perryville I had made a start. It pleased me to have found so many home-cooked meals on the road, and to have been able to enjoy the conversations of strangers, because in the motels and at the waffle houses there were none. Later I came across the phrase "a confederacy of the mind," which captures my affection for Appalachia.

For souvenirs I had those wrought-iron hooks and nails from the Hillsboro café, some jam from Lexington, salt from Saltville (of course), and a stack of books and images that would keep alive the clearing where Lee and Jackson planned the flanking attack or Robert Kennedy held his hearings in Appalachia. Mostly what I appreciated was that, when the court hearings resumed on Monday, I could put a commercial dispute in the context of far greater suffering. All I had to do was answer tough questions from lawyers and listen to well paid executives say, "I don't recall."

Leaving the Wilderness, unsure about whether to go forward to Richmond or back across the Rappahannock, Grant had faced a more difficult dilemma. Either way he turned, the results would have been deadly, to the Union cause or his men. He chose to go forward, saying: "I propose to fight it out on this line if it takes all summer," a sentiment that can work as well in lawsuits as in war.

During the months that followed my return, as I listened to objections about objections, at least I could allow my mind to wander back and forth across the contours of American history, wondering just how much of it was out of range in acoustical shadows or what lies down the road or over that next hill.